MW01087818

Melinda —

A

SACRED

DUTY

How a Whistleblower took on the VA and won

PAULA PEDENE
WITH **DOUG WILLIAMS**

Thank you for being a life long friend to Bell and a decades long friend to me. We are so grateful to have you in our lives! ♡ Love you Paula Pedene

Skyrocket Press
28020 Newbird Drive
Santa Clarita, CA 91350
www.SkyrocketPress.com

Cover Art Design by Wayne Slaten
Final Cover Design by Barbara Groves @
www.BrokenCandleBookDesigns.com
Interior Design by Laurisa Reyes

ISBN: 978-1-947394-04-9

Some names have been changed to protect those persons' identities.

A
SACRED
DUTY

How a Whistleblower took on the VA and won

PAULA PEDENE
WITH **DOUG WILLIAMS**

Santa Clarita, CA

What People Are Saying about
A Sacred Duty...

"This is a story of how far the federal bureaucracy will go to crush someone who threatens it. Paula fought back against a system that was rigged against her. Her story is both frightening and enraging, but ultimately inspiring." – Pete Hegseth, *Fox & Friends*

"Every now and then, justice prevails and the little people win, while the 'empowered folks' lose it all. Caring for veterans is the job, not cooking the books for personal gain. Fortunately, some people still know that, and Paula is one of them." - Dr. Sam Foote, retired VA Physician & Phoenix VA Whistleblower

---

"Veteran lives were at risk. Nobody would listen. Entrenched bureaucrats thought they could bury the scandal. Paula Pedene knew different." – Congressman Jeff Miller

---

"At its core, *A Sacred Duty* is Paula's journey as a Whistleblower. She takes us through the ordeal of when she found herself at war with an institution bent on erasing her. More than that, however, in confronting this particular Goliath, Paula Pedene discovered the David within her." – Roger French, Employee Representative & retired Veterans Affairs HR Director

---

"(Paula Pedene) was a 20-year employee at the hospital who oversaw everything from news releases to the hospital newsletter to the annual

Veterans Day Parade. In 2010, Pedene joined a group that complained to VA's upper management about the Phoenix hospital's director. They alleged that the director had allowed budget shortfalls and berated subordinates. And it seemed to work. VA's inspector general investigated and found an $11 million shortfall in the hospital's budget. The director retired voluntarily. 'I felt we had actually done the right thing,' Pedene said. But that turned out to be the beginning of her troubles, not the end." – David Fahrenthold, *The Washington Post*, August 3, 2014

"The VA has a mission of life and death consequences for America's veterans. Unfortunately, its coverups of mismanagement and corruption have betrayed the foundation principle of medicine: First, do no harm. Even worse, it is number one in government retaliation against whistleblowers who defend patients. The VA generates from 33-40% of whistleblower retaliation complaints annually. In a warm, down to earth manner, Paula Pedene speaks from the heart about how much it cost to successfully defend her principles. She is the invisible hero whose whistleblowing pioneered exposure of a national medical care breakdown. As a result, her life was a multi-year waking nightmare. She speaks from the heart about the anguish, frustration and stress from relentless retaliation. For anyone who wants to know the facts of life about being a public servant trying to make a difference in a hostile bureaucracy – read this book!" – Tom Devine, Legal Director, Government Accountability Project

This book is dedicated to
Bill, Robert, and Steven.
I love you forever.

TABLE OF CONTENTS

1

A Day Like No Other

April 9, 2014 began like any other day for me. Well, like any other day since I'd been sentenced to purgatory in the library of the Phoenix Veterans Affairs Health Care System (PVAHCS). But this day would end like no other.

I went upstairs to get the daily paper, the *Arizona Republic*, smiling and saying hello to a few folks along the way. Some smiled back. That was a far cry from much of the previous year when many of my colleagues refused to meet my eye or, if they did, looked at me as if I were some kind of Judas. If you're an accused security risk and charged with "serious allegations of misconduct," people tend to believe the worst. When hospital leadership rules by fear, and a whistleblower stands up to take them on, allies are hard to come by.

Anyway, after I retrieved the paper, I took my long journey back to the library, dreading each step. For some reason, I suddenly felt the full weight of the past sixteen months burdening me once more. Some of it had lifted over time, as the occasional positive newspaper story appeared, or if my representatives scored wins against the monolithic bureaucracy that was the Department of Veterans Affairs (VA). But what had begun as a bogus 30-day investigation of me back in December of 2012 had now stretched out to almost a year and a half, and the end was still nowhere in sight. My legal bills were stacking up. My family was unraveling. My depression was deepening. My emails were being monitored. The higher-ups were doing everything in their considerable power to force me out. And despite many, many letters and phone calls to VA in Washington, no one was paying any attention. It felt like I was reliving a nightmare.

Back in the library, I returned to business as usual: checking people onto the computers; making photocopies for the veterans; faxing their documents; letting them use the phone; sharpening their pencils; checking books in and out; helping staff find the medical literature research they needed; reshelving books; ensuring forms were signed and training credits were captured; and preparing for an upcoming continuing education forum, where I was the administrative point person. It wasn't rocket science, but it was what a Temporary Library Technician (my new "title") did. It was a far cry from what I'd been doing before Sharon Helman and Lance Robinson, the top two executives at the hospital, had forced me from my position as Public Affairs Officer and orchestrated a campaign to smear me professionally and personally, but my job was to perform my duties, no matter how mundane. That's what members of the military do, and I was a decorated Navy veteran honorably discharged, and then re-enlisted during Operation Desert Storm. The fact that my library job was drudgery was not relevant.

As I went through my tasks, about the only thing that would break the monotony was taking a few minutes to watch a House Veterans Affairs Committee hearing later in the day. I'd cleared it with my supervisor because, by that time, I cleared everything.

Even my bathroom breaks. The length and frequency of those trips were monitored, too.

For the first hour and a half of the hearing, nothing earthshaking happened. Then U.S. Representative Jeff Miller of Florida, the committee chairman, began to question Dr. Thomas Lynch, who was the Assistant Deputy Under Secretary for Health for Clinical Operations at the Department of Veterans Affairs. Congressman Miller told Dr. Lynch that the next topic was "unofficial wait lists at the Phoenix VA." Dr. Lynch seemed unfazed by the fact, but he didn't know what the chairman knew, the secrets that I and my friend and fellow whistleblower Dr. Sam Foote knew, and the secrets that my superiors at the Phoenix VA had tried so hard to conceal – through intimidation, harassment, data manipulations, sham investigations, and the threat of career-ending personnel sanctions: *Executives at the medical center had engaged in a conspiracy and cover-up that was killing our veterans.*

Congressman Miller eyed Dr. Lynch. Even on a computer monitor, and even though I am legally blind, I could see the restrained anger in his face. A moment passed. Then he asked a question that would bring down the house of lies that Sharon, Lance, and their confederates had so cruelly constructed:

"It appears as though there could be as many as forty veterans whose deaths could be related to delays in care. Were you made aware of any of this in your lookback?"

Winston Churchill once famously said, "A lie gets halfway around the world before the truth has a chance to get its pants on." On April 9, 2014, however, it was the truth that would rocket not just halfway around the world but all over the world.

One of the darkest episodes in VA history would be exposed.

The dominoes would fall.

Finally.

2

FROM STELLAR CARE TO SCANDAL

T he Department of Veterans Affairs is a sprawling institution. It has more than 1,700 hospitals, clinics, and related facilities; over 375,000 employees; and an annual budget of about $180 billion. It is the federal government's second-largest Cabinet-level agency.

In recent years, as the controversies over its failings have surfaced, veterans' advocates said it was crippled by, among other things, bureaucratic behavior that put ambition and pursuit of personal power over the welfare of the men and women who served our country. I agree with the accusation. I have been a victim of that mindset. But I cannot and will not personally plead guilty to the charge.

Working with veterans has never been just a job for me. It's been a lifelong commitment, at least in my adult years. I was in the U.S. Navy from 1978 to 1986, and then re-enlisted five years later to support the operations in the Middle East. During my career in and out of the service, I earned some decorations; co-anchored the nationally broadcast TV show *Navy News This Week*;

and was a news reporter at the Far East Network in Tokyo and at Broadcast Detachment 27 on Midway Island. After the Navy, I worked on a freelance basis for Cox Broadcasting, *Potomac News*, and PBS, the latter on a show titled *For Veterans Only*. Later, I was hired by the State Department's U.S. Information Agency as a broadcast news anchor and reporter for its television show *America Today*.

That's professional stuff, though. I'm proud of it, don't get me wrong, but I'm not the type to leave my dedication at the desk when five o'clock rolls around.

In 2008-2009, I collaborated with U.S. Rep. Harry Mitchell on legislation to give Congressional Medal of Honor recipients priority status for receiving eligibility for their VA health care. Unfortunately, they had been overlooked when Congress established the "enrollment categories" for VA health care. We found out when a wonderful colleague of mine, Congressional Medal of Honor recipient Fred Ferguson, took me up on my advice to get care at the Phoenix VA. Rectifying this oversight was a "no brainer" to myself and Congressman Mitchell. The passage of the Medal of Honor Health Care Equity Act is one I'm proud to have seen come to light.

With support from others, I created two nonprofits, the Veterans Medical Leadership Council and Honoring America's Veterans. The first provides support to veterans in their transition home from the military. The second provides honor and recognition through special events like the Phoenix Veterans Day Parade. That Parade, which I created, has now become one of the largest in attendance in the nation. Little did I know, it would become a pawn in VA's strategy to silence and intimidate me.

I share these successes not out of ego. Lord knows, there are hundreds – check that, thousands – of good, skilled professionals in VA with comparable if not better resumés, and a whole lot of military folks with service records that dwarf mine. I simply wish to make the point that working on behalf of the military, and with veterans in particular, is not some 20-and-out, retire, and collect-a-pension deal with me. It's what I live for.

And that makes everything that followed so painful and outrageous.

I came to the Phoenix Veterans Affairs Health Care System in 1994. At the time, it was named after our long serving Senator Carl T. Hayden, who personally advocated with constituents to build the hospital. The name changed in 2007, but I digress. During my tenure there as the first full-time Public Affairs Officer, we were experiencing phenomenal growth. The Southwest had become a mecca for veterans. We grew the hospital from its basic inpatient model to one that now has ten community care clinics serving more than 91,000 veterans in Arizona. As PAO, I was proud to help highlight the center as a model of excellence and efficiency with compassionate and superior care – because it was. For most of the first twenty years of my tenure at Phoenix, we maintained that level of skill and integrity.

But by 2011, it had become a nightmare. I know that sounds harsh, and in no way is it a reflection of the stellar employees who worked there – the doctors, nurses, staff, and volunteers who had brought the hospital acclaim across the nation.

No, the problem was the arrival of new senior leaders. And just like that, I mean almost overnight, what had been a caring environment mutated into a hostile workplace. Management put targets on the backs of people they didn't like or who had the nerve to push back against their "new" procedures that even on their best day were questionable. Women were harassed, and staff members were intimidated and threatened almost daily. Backbiting was rampant. It was evident that the pursuit of absolute power – especially power over people – became more important to those who held it than did the welfare of our veterans.

You know what they say about absolute power, right? It corrupts absolutely. The Phoenix VA was the poster child for that. By the end of 2011, it was in open conflict (including swords, but more on that later). A few of us thought if we fought back and took their power away, we'd get back to the business of caring for our nation's veterans.

We were wrong. None of us knew how wrong until it became obvious the situation was only going to get worse, and that the battle was just beginning.

And in this battle, people were actually going to die.

3
DARKNESS DESCENDS

I t's difficult, and maybe a little unfair, to point to one incident or individual and say, "That's why things went wrong." Typically, failure percolates over time, under the surface, until it suddenly blooms into something that's as horrible as it is tragic.

That wasn't the case in Phoenix. As I've said, the hospital had for years been a model of care and compassion for veterans. Then Geoff Reyes* arrived as director, and Carter Beam* as his No. 2. Almost instantly, everything changed, and a years-long darkness began to settle over the medical center.

Reyes didn't care for me from the start. I'm not sure why, though more than a few theories have surfaced. I have a severe vision problem that has rendered me legally blind, which some said made me an easy target. Also, I was never afraid to speak my mind when I thought doing so was in the best interests of the hospital or the veterans. Reyes could not abide a woman with opinions, let alone one who voiced them. I even heard suggestions that I intimidated him. Yeah, right. I'm a little over 5 feet tall, I walk with a white cane, and I prefer spas and wine to gyms and protein shakes. Duane "The Rock" Johnson I'm not.

But whatever the reason, I was in Reyes's sites. I don't think I was being paranoid. Like they said in the ads for that movie *Enemy of the State* (which, ironically, I would become), "It's not paranoia if they're really after you." And Reyes was really after me.

Some of it was small stuff. I'm convinced it was designed to show he could keep me in line when he wanted. Between Reyes and Beam, they wouldn't approve my leave requests until the last possible minute, making planning almost impossible. They actively solicited criticism of me by staff so they could use it later, something the two had also done to one of my colleagues, Susan Young* (a woman, surprise!). Susan was the Assistant Chief of Health Administration Service and an eight-year Army veteran. Beam went so far as to smack her on the rear end once with a spatula. It was reprehensible.

These moves against us were a pain, and it was insulting, and honestly, if you're going to paint a target on someone, you ought to be smart enough not to be so obvious. They weren't. Both were so transparent (and not in the good way). Then Beam upped the ante by deciding to pull responsibility for the Phoenix VA's Veterans Day Parade away from me. He reached out to his "executive assistant" and asked him if he thought he could handle the Parade along with his other duties, as Beam thought that I might be moving to "another role." Not only did the assistant decline, (seeing it, and rightly so, as a massive increase in workload), but his assistant also threatened to leave Phoenix if the Parade was reassigned to him. Beam decided his assistant wasn't the right choice for the job, so he laid in wait for another opportunity.

This may not seem like much of a big deal, but the Parade matters to Phoenix and to the veterans it honors. It matters to me, too, and Beam knew it. That's why he wanted it out of my hands. It wouldn't be the last time someone tried to weaponize the Parade as a tool of retaliation against me.

By way of background, Arizona has about 500,000 veterans, and the Phoenix Parade is the largest in the state – and the fourth largest in attendance in the country. While it is certainly an All-American, red-white-and-blue event that spotlights the role brave men and women have played in protecting our freedoms, it also has an impact that goes far beyond celebration of the military.

One Korean War veteran said, "After being a grand marshal in the Parade, the demons I faced every night in my dreams were gone." A member of the Navy who served in Operation Enduring Freedom echoed that: "Words cannot describe what the Parade and being a grand marshal did for me. It's beyond anything else in helping me heal."

I created the Parade in 1997 and have been its coordinator for over twenty years. It is very much a part of my identity among veterans and within the community as a whole. To arbitrarily yank it from my duties, for no reason other than because Carter Beam wanted to humiliate me, speaks volumes about him and the culture of hostility and harassment that had come to pervade our hospital. That he didn't succeed speaks equal volumes about how much he overestimated his power and underestimated the impact my removal would have on veterans and the staff.

Now to some people, what Beam did might be seen as petty and mean-spirited (yep and yep), but he was an altar boy compared to his boss.

Geoff Reyes came to Phoenix in 2009 and served as both head of the hospital and as its Equal Employment Opportunity officer – a designation that, as we'll see in a second, is the irony of ironies.

I'm going to try and separate what I think about him, which, trust me, is not very flattering, from what I witnessed or heard first-hand. But to be sure, that was just as unflattering and speaks for itself.

Put simply, Reyes seemed to think he was a king, though narcissist might be a more apt description. He remodeled the director's office suite and turned it into plush, lavish, expensive digs that included a $7,000 shower. On at least two occasions, he appeared to use hospital resources to cater and throw theme parties at his home. Not for the enjoyment of the entire staff, but only for selected employees. If an invitee failed to attend, their standing with the director plummeted.

Once, just before the beginning of a Research and Development meeting, Reyes grabbed the hand of a woman without asking, pulled her up from the table, and said he was going to teach her a Mexican dance. He did, too, for the next minute or so. The woman was embarrassed. I would be, too. What does a Mexican dance have to do with R&D? This was mild, though, compared to the time he sat down at the table with an attractive female employee and started talking about "organisms" – but instead kept saying "orgasms." Funny guy.

Now, about those swords.

We had a sign at the hospital that said no guns, knives, or weapons of any kind were allowed inside. They're posted at just about every patient entrance at the medical center. Obviously, the goal was to ensure patient and employee safety, and it applied to all of us.

All of us, that is, except Geoff Reyes.

He kept a pair of foils on display in his office. That's a pretty bold and blatant violation of the rules, but Reyes took it one step beyond. He would actually invite people to duel with him. I'm not kidding. He'd pull the swords down, hand one to the unfortunate soul who happened to be there, and go into full-on Errol Flynn mode. I can only imagine the scene if he'd had dueling pistols. We'd have to call in a SWAT team.

I was never on his Top Ten List of favorite people, but like most VA employees at the time, I kept my head down and tried to go through the recognized channels to affect some kind of change. Good luck with that.

Then something happened that pushed me over the edge.

We were at a staff meeting and were discussing an advertising campaign to promote free flu shots for our veterans. Reyes wanted the campaign to start immediately, as in right that second. I politely questioned him, noting that the first shipment of vaccine wasn't due for four weeks, and if we advertised for people to come in now, it would only result in a lot of them making the trip for no reason. Everybody but Reyes agreed, and thanks to the majority, the campaign was delayed.

The next day, the vaccine arrived unexpectedly. You'd have thought it was Christmas morning, and Santa had left him a train set.

"I was right!" Reyes announced at a meeting two days later. He went on with a tirade that attacked my competence as a professional, my judgment, and my ability to meet the requirements of my job description (blindness, you understand, was always a default rationale for these guys). At the end, he was wagging his forearm back and forth, pointing at me, and saying, "Next time, you do what I say!"

Okay, it's confession time, so let me be very honest here.

The week before Reyes's gleeful tirade, Dr. Sam Foote – a no-nonsense physician who ran the VA's Thunderbird Clinic and would become a central figure in exposing the scandal that followed three years later – came to me with a request. "We need to do something," he said. "We need to tell someone what this guy is doing and how it is hurting morale and undercutting patient care."

I told him no, I couldn't help. I had a mortgage, two kids prepping for college, and a job I needed to keep until I could retire. Given the climate at Phoenix VA, I just could not afford the risk.

Then, after Reyes dressed me down for the flu shots in front of everyone, Sam asked again. He'd seen the tirade on the video conference. He called me and asked for my home phone number. I said, "Sam, I trust you, but why do you need my home number?"

"Paula, if I was in the room today, I would have clocked him."

"Oh Sam, you can definitely have my home phone number."

Thus, our collaboration began.

Call it "Revenge of the Blind Girl" if you will, I don't care. Reyes was hurting morale. Everyone knew it.

On Feb. 13, 2011, Sam sent a letter – which I helped him write – to the VA's Inspector General Hotline in Washington, detailing all of this. Never one to mince words, he said, "He (Reyes) alone bears the primary responsibility for the implosion of our medical center. He is a self-promoting, arrogant, narcissistic micromanager whose ignorance is only exceeded by his incompetence." The letter included a laundry list of actions, and inactions, by Reyes – from not filling key positions, to saddling the facility with out-of-date supplies, to making veterans wait for hours to see a doctor, to cutting costs on community care while spending lavishly on himself.

While he was building that $7,000 shower and his own personal McMansion office and throwing command-performance parties serving umbrella drinks, Reyes was dragging a great hospital down a financial hole.

There had been whispers, some louder than others, that the Phoenix VA Health Care System had experienced a serious multi-million-dollar budget shortfall in Fiscal 2010. This was due to mismanagement of the Non-VA Fee Care program, which covers the medical costs for veterans who sought care in the community when they couldn't get the care they needed at a VA facility. Sam and I pointed fingers in that direction, and VA investigators followed, attributing the loss to poor management, lax oversight, and ineffective processes. The mismanagement included ineffective authorization procedures because clinical managers did not adequately monitor approved and appropriate levels of fee care requests. It's poor care.

This may not sound like much, but the price tag was staggering: $11.4 million.

The problem – for Reyes and the hospital – was that he had not allocated enough money in the budget for the "fee basis" care. So, the hospital had to go out and get $2.3 million in special funding from VA's national Fee Care Program and another $5.4 million in supplemental funding. Oh, and the Phoenix VA canceled $3.8 million in planned equipment purchases.

Let me be blunt: Reyes had to go, and the letter Sam and I put together helped push him out the door.

By the end of 2011, after a pretty scathing report from the VA Office of the Inspector General and a few more support letters, both Reyes and Beam were gone. With new leadership on the way, I felt like the hospital was turning the corner, that we'd get back to our primary mission of supporting veterans, and that my fight against a hostile work environment and the powers-that-be was in the in the past.

Boy, was I wrong.

The fight was just beginning. And it seems as if the prior leaders were rank amateurs compared to who was lying in wait for me.

4
HARDLY A NEW BEGINNING

With Reyes and Beam out of the picture, you could almost feel the sense of relief that settled in at the Phoenix VA. The long hospital nightmare was over. Everyone was looking forward to a reset, the kind of new beginning that would let us close the book on the problems of the old administration and keep our focus back where it belonged – on the veterans.

Initially, Lance Robinson was assigned to cover for one of the leadership vacancies as interim Associate Director. He was about 5'11" with brown hair and a medium stocky build. On paper, he looked like someone with a lot of potential. He'd worked his way up the VA leadership chain, serving five years in Salt Lake City and three in Amarillo before coming to Phoenix, and he had a pretty deep background in health administration – an important function at a hospital. So, he knew about things like patient billing, scheduling, and process flow. Like I said, he checked a bunch of boxes.

But looks can be deceiving.

15

From my point of view, he was also a bully who would become known for trying to intimidate employees with threats that could peel paint off the ceiling. (I know. I peeled a lot.) At a time when we should have been doing whatever it took to restore morale, he focused on other things, including how to keep a hold of the position. Basically, it appeared as if Lance did exactly what he wanted to do, exactly how he wanted to do it, and said the hell with everyone and everything else. To most of us, his approach to administration or management or employee relations – and looking back, I wouldn't put any of those terms in the same sentence with "Lance Robinson" – could be boiled down to seven words: "The flogging will continue until morale improves."

He got it half right. The flogging did continue. Morale, though, was another matter.

And that made him the perfect No. 2 for Sharon Helman.

Sharon was appointed the Medical Center Director in early 2012, with Lance officially taking the position of Associate Director. Sharon was a rising star in the VA system, moving up from Spokane – where her service was praised by no less than U.S. Sen. Patty Murray, who called her skills at problem-solving and communication "unparalleled" (pause for irony, Part 1) – to a highly complex hospital in Chicago. Sharon was hard to miss. Blonde, blue-eyed, standing about 5 foot 5, and a flashy dresser, she favored skirts that always struck me as a bit too short and heels that were more than a bit too high.

Sharon cultivated her standing in VA circles well and was likely setting her sites on getting to Washington D.C. in some type of higher role. In a VA email bulletin dated March 4, 2012, she described her vision of leadership: "I base my decisions on three things, first is it good for the veteran, second is it good for the staff, and third is it good for the family – mine and our VA family.

If we can answer yes, then I know that this is the best thing we can be doing."

The platitudes didn't stop there:

"This is about how we care for our veterans like we care for our own family."

"I am your team; we are all in this together."

"What I expect of you, I expect of myself."

"I want you all taking risks because when we do, we succeed as a team, and if we fail, we fail as a team, since we are all taking these risks together."

(Pause for irony, Part 2.)

Hearing all that, you can understand why I was excited by her assignment. Also, she was the first female director in the hospital's sixty-year history, and I'll admit to feeling proud about that. I was looking forward to building a strong working relationship with her. Then three things happened that should have put me, the hospital, and VA on full alert.

First, I was provided with documents showing her husband was being placed on the medical center payroll. That was a violation of nepotism rules and personnel practice laws under the department's Office of Personnel Management and Office of Special Counsel. It was a red flag, to be sure, but it was also odd as it made her seem as if the policies that affected the rest of us did not apply to her.

Second, she moved to boost employee productivity, which is understandable and crucial in any organization, but she did it in ways that were miles from understandable. Staff started complaining that their performance reviews were suddenly lowered, according to new standards that they didn't know about, weren't trained on, and had never served under. By law, employees are not supposed to be rated for at least ninety days when new standards are put in place. The staff began feeling upset and angry all over again.

Third, there was me.

In March 2012, Sharon asked for a public affairs briefing. It didn't seem out of the ordinary; she had seen some of my work and how I managed meetings and events, and seemed to appreciate them, and I had briefed Lance the previous December. So, I went in fully prepared to give her a bigger-picture look at the public affairs operation, a deeper dive into what we do, and offer some thoughts on how we could help achieve her mission for the hospital. In retrospect, I was probably naïve because my little corner of the hospital was the last thing she wanted to hear about.

No, Sharon claimed the purpose of the meeting was to get background on the public affairs program, and to inquire about facts and circumstances regarding previous hospital leadership. But not *just* that. During the conversation she also asked me about the role I played in causing their departures. I later realized this wasn't a briefing. It was intelligence gathering.

The war of whistleblower retaliation was about to begin.

5
SHARPENING THE AX

On Jan. 6, 2012, I mistakenly emailed a document containing personal information, including names and addresses, of 71,467 veterans to about seventy-five members of the Public Relations Society of America, Masters Special Interest Group. It is a professional organization that I am deeply involved with. It was an innocent mistake, and totally my fault.

So how did that happen?

First, I need to tell you about my eyesight. When I was in the Navy, they discovered I had an eye disease called Retinitis Pigmentosa. The disease causes pigment to form on the retina, they are not sure if it is from the photo receptor cells dying and leaving pigment or what, but I had it. As the pigment continues to build over time, it literally causes tunnel vision. The pigment blocks the receptor cells on the periphery of the retina, removing vision from the side, top and down. What remains is the central vision only. Fortunately, my sight during my enlistment was still strong, so I was able to finish my first tour of duty and reenlist for a second tour of duty. I left the Navy after two tours, when I started dating my husband. He was an officer, and I was enlisted, and even though we weren't in the same chain of command, the optics didn't look good. I later joined the Reserves when Operation Desert Storm started as I still wanted to serve. At that point, Bill and I were married, so we had to ensure we worked at separate commands. He was stationed at the Buffalo NY Reserve Center, so I would travel to Willow Grove, PA to be with my unit. After three and a half years, when my enlistment was up, they found my vision had deteriorated to the point where I couldn't reenlist. I was bummed, but I picked myself up and moved on. I turned to the VA, and they provided me with training to adjust, including no more driving, walking with a white cane, having more true-to-light lights installed in my office and home, and learning adaptive skills on the computer. All of it helped, and I would often ask to try new setups to see if it would improve my work environment.

Which brings me back to where I left off, with the email of names going to outsiders, (I still cringe about it to this day). I had just been given two computer screens to help me with some of the eyesight issues I was facing. One monitor was set up by IRM for me to read my email inbox, which was always overflowing. I'd get as many as 1,500 messages a week, and often had to spend Saturdays and Sundays catching up. The other monitor allowed me to focus on whatever work product was on my plate at the moment. I could keep multiple projects on the monitors at once, so I wouldn't have to reduce their size to cram the information onto just one.

On this particular day, the work product in question was the mailing list for the hospital's patient newsletter. I was getting ready to upload the patient list to a secure server, so I could coordinate the distribution of the patient newsletter, through a vendor. After

I'd spot-checked the file on one monitor to be sure it was ready to go, I uploaded it and went to my email screen on the other monitor, where I was finishing a note about an upcoming PRSA event we'd be hosting at the hospital. I hit SEND to get that out and almost immediately received a "privacy notice email" stating it appeared I had shared information that could be considered as "protected patient information."

I went back into my SENT folder and was mortified to discover that I had somehow inadvertently attached the patient mailing list to the PRSA group email.

I'm going to admit something here.

After I realized what had happened, I went outside and had a long talk with myself. There was a moment when I thought, Paula, just let it slide. Don't tell anyone. Nobody will ever find out. No harm, no foul. Then I'd tell myself, well, if it's not so bad, why did you get the privacy notice? I went back and forth like this in my head for a few minutes, and when I'd finished the tormenting internal dialogue, I decided, Nope, you made a mistake, and you're better off owning up to it.

I realized that it represented a potential privacy violation, and I could face some disciplinary action. I may be independent and unafraid to speak my mind, but I also tend to follow the rules. And even though there is a lot of gray area between government rules and public relations (like, is it okay to use federal funds for community outreach? And how is outreach defined and determined?), this wasn't a PR issue. It was about patient privacy, something we take very seriously at VA, and I had sent what we call personally identifiable information to a list of people who weren't supposed to see it. Like I said, that was on me, and that's why I "put myself on report," the consequences be damned.

I called the hospital's two privacy officers and told them what happened. One of them was Kim Tesh* who I knew would go running to Lance. She did indeed go running, and when she told him what I'd done, I was trembling.

Lance called me into his office and chewed me out as only Lance could. He asked me questions about almost every person on the PRSA list, wanting to know if they would use the patient information, or the fact that I'd distributed it, against us. After I assured him they wouldn't, he ordered me to do a full recovery – to get 100 percent of the emails back – and have that action verified.

It took a few days, with both Lance and the privacy folks breathing down my neck, but we did it. I plodded through each email, one by one, asking people to delete it. Then I called to ensure they did. If I couldn't reach someone because they had changed jobs, I'd call their supervisor, who would put me in touch with IT to ensure the email couldn't be recovered. If people were out on vacation, I'd call friends to get their numbers. You get the gist. I was embarrassed to ask my public relations colleagues to help, but I took the hit for my error and did what was necessary. In the end, we were able to verify a 100% recall, and the privacy officers closed this one out.

Even though I'd done exactly as ordered, Lance wouldn't let it go. I don't think it was really about the accidental release of patient information. By this point in time, it was becoming more evident that both he and Sharon didn't want me in the Public Affairs Officer (PAO) role. I say this because I had also received a call from Sharon's former PAO in Chicago asking me if I'd consider taking the Executive Assistant to the Director job to Sharon, so I could "broaden my experience" and in turn, she could move to Phoenix. I suggested that she take the EA job since she could report directly to Sharon and help her from there, but of course she declined. Nonetheless, it didn't stop them from trying to force a change, including using the "privacy incident" as a reason. There was just one problem for them with this strategy.

Security officials at VA headquarters ruled the email disclosure was in fact an inadvertent policy violation that did not merit discipline. Unfortunately for Lance and Sharon, that meant it was not a major data breach that would require public disclosure and notifications. When Lance heard the news, he argued that the incident jeopardized the personal security of thousands of veterans and should not be covered up to avert a public relations disaster. He saw the whole thing as leverage. But with a "no breach ruling" he needed something else, something bigger, to sharpen his ax for the next swing.

In November 2012, he found it:

My husband.

6

THE PLOT TAKES SHAPE

L ance wasn't going to give up easily after VA security determined my accidental email was inadvertent rather than a data breach. As 2012 continued, it became more and more obvious he wasn't going to give up on "getting me" at all.

I'm a workhorse. I never tried to hide it, and that put a lot of stress on me to do the job and do it right, but the previous few years were beginning to wear on me. I had gone from four staff and a healthy budget, down to two staff and a minimal budget. A year earlier, Lance was supposed to help restore my budget and staff, as recommended by the director of the Veterans Integrated Service Network (VISN), which oversees the region that included Phoenix. Instead, he found ways to make sure that never happened. He used the fact that I would push myself as far as needed to get everything done to hurt me. I have little doubt that he not only knew about my need to keep everything in step no matter the cost, but I also believe he wanted to use it as a weapon to force me out. Routinely, I saw evidence where he was working

24

to create an environment where my performance would suffer, giving him some "justification" for firing me.

Here is some of what happened:

Starting in April, he'd call me to his office, forcing me to walk an eighth of a mile from my building to his. Then he'd make me wait twenty or so minutes only to cancel the meeting due to other "pressing" issues, or just not show up. A lot of these meetings were late in the day, meaning that I'd miss my vanpool ride home. Several months later, he decided to move me to his building so he could be "more in touch" with his public affairs officer (Translation, Part 1: to keep an eye on me) and had me lugging my office stuff across the medical center's campus in the hottest part of the year. After the move, he would pop into my office, unannounced, for an arbitrary tongue-lashing. He often did it in the presence of others, compounding my humiliation. (Translation, Part 2: easier to humiliate me around my colleagues.)

Adding insult to injury, and just when I thought I was making some progress on staffing and budget issues, Lance denied restoration of the public affairs function and even went so far as to demand that I look at further program reductions instead. He also refused to give me the staff necessary to support the functions of my office.

Then, out of the blue, he indicated in August that he was going to take responsibility for the Veterans Day Parade away from me and told me to keep overtime and weekend work to a minimum. Of course, he knew full well that I handled my work overload during off hours at no pay, and that much of my coordination of the Parade was on my time, not the hospital's. He also knew that I typically didn't request overtime pay for any of these activities. As far as I was concerned, they were part of the job.

(Oh, and get this. Sharon once sent Lance an email complaining, "Paula is working on the weekend." Think about that for a second. The head of the hospital is telling her No. 2 that I'm doing my job, unpaid, on my own time, which for the record I was working on *her* column for the employee newsletter to meet a deadline. But come on. With all the problems the hospital was facing, she was paying attention to my unpaid work time. Seriously?)

What this all adds up to is that Lance was demanding I do the job with both hands – budgetary and personnel – tied behind my back.

Then he started trying to use my eyesight against me.

He began to openly ask me about my retirement plans, pushing me to consider leaving the hospital due to my disability, something that was so wrong on so many levels. Then he demanded that I have a "reasonable accommodation audit." In the government, they're so receptive to hiring people with disabilities, who can function with minimal impairment, that there are several programs to protect us. The "reasonable accommodation" is one of them. It's designed to make sure you have the equipment, space, and any needed work adjustments to ensure the disability doesn't get in the way. I had been assessed years before, and nothing had changed with my eyesight issues, so I knew an audit was unnecessary. Not according to Lance, though. I had to sit there and go through an assessment. I was insulted and humiliated, under the gaze of a safety specialist person, but I did prove that I could answer a phone, file folders in a cabinet, and walk from one corner of my office to the other, and I could still see the computer monitor to do my job. Lance claimed it was necessary because my vision might have worsened, even though I had told him it was stable, and my doctor had written a letter verifying that.

I passed the evaluation. My guess is that Lance was less than thrilled. He didn't care one iota about my sight. He was looking for a reason to force me out because he had no foundation to do it based on my job performance.

But Lance wasn't just playing games with my job performance and disability at this point. I could sense he was about to take his bully act to new heights.

One time, at the end of November, I told him I'd heard that my budget – already slashed – was going to be cut by an additional twenty-five percent the following year. He demanded to know how I had found this out, as I hadn't yet had my official budget briefing. The environment at Phoenix VA being what it was, with everyone afraid they were going to lose their jobs, I was concerned that revealing my source would have negatively impacted my colleague who had given me the information.

When I refused to tell Lance who it was, he exploded, getting so mad and so loud that I had to ask if we needed to bring in a mediator for any future talks. He backed off, but I was still afraid he would try to drum up a way to use the episode against me. Still shaken by the encounter, I checked with my employee representative, Roger French, who told me it was a requirement, per human resources guidelines, to share the name of the person who'd given me the information. The next morning, I walked into Lance's office to tell him. At first, he seemed almost relieved. There was none of the hostile bluster that passed for his management style, but it was the calm before the storm. In an instant, he went ballistic again, calling me a liar, threatening to discipline me for a "lack of candor," and saying I was guilty of "misleading a supervisor in conversation after a direct request was made."

Maybe it was his paranoia. Maybe he believed in conspiracies. Maybe it was part of some grand strategy he and Sharon had cooked up. I don't know. What I do know, however, is that he was pushing me closer and closer to the edge.

There was something else I didn't know: His plot for getting rid of me was already in the works by this time.

With my budget and staff cut, I often had to rely on registered, unpaid volunteers to get the work done. My husband Bill was one of them. A year prior, he had volunteered to help at the hospital in its medical media department, as he had a degree in cinematography from the University of Southern California. So, here's this guy who's great at film, photography, and creativity – all assets I needed but I wasn't getting from medical media (thanks, Lance) – who was ready to volunteer to help somehow, some way. Rather than keeping him busy in medical media, the chief decided to assign him to support me, and for several months, Bill was helping me with photo shoots and other creative venues.

A bit about my hubby.

He had served admirably in the Navy for twenty years as a Surface Warfare Officer, racking up Navy Achievement medals for superior service. He is a reserved man, and my rock. He took on the role of "stay-at-home" dad so I could pour myself into my job, and he worked as a substitute teacher and photographer when he could.

When we first met, his blonde hair (now gray) glistened. He was a Lieutenant on shore duty at Anacostia Naval Station in Washington, D.C., and I was there too, as a Petty Officer First Class and Navy journalist, working as the first female news anchor for the Navy's television show, *Navy News This Week*. I planned to get out of the Navy later that year, go to San Diego State University, and pursue a master's degree and a broadcasting career as a civilian. You know what they say about making plans, right? It's what you do to make God laugh.

Our first interaction in March 1986 was anything but romantic. I was walking down the hallway where we both worked, and he said, "Petty Office LeClaire, I know you."

"I'm sorry, sir," I replied politely, "but I don't know you."

"I've watched your shows when I was at sea," he said.

Then it dawned on me: Oh, that's right. Outside of my bubble in D.C., people on ships at sea and around the world were watching the show. So, I guess my reach maybe did go beyond a broadcast studio. At least it made its way to Bill, anyway.

I looked at him thinking, Oh, boy, this one's cute and intriguing.

We started dating quietly a few months later. I say "quietly," as he was an officer and I was enlisted, and we didn't want to get caught up in the "aura of fraternization" that is frowned upon in the military. He wasn't my supervisor, nor was he in my chain of command. I left the Navy at the end of my enlistment in September but remained in Washington to keep dating Bill. After a year, I was still wondering about my plans for San Diego and what to do with Bill, as I knew it was getting serious. Then one Sunday at Mass, in the chapel where John and Jacqueline Kennedy got married, I knew what to do. Not because I figured it out, but because these "cupid-like angels" appeared and told me to go to him, saying, "This is a good thing." It was a clear sign that my strategy to land in San Diego was about to be detoured – all for the good. Bill and I were married a year later.

But I digress.

Bill was helping me with photography and other support as a registered VA volunteer, while our kids were at school.

After the Veterans Day Parade on Monday, Nov. 12, (we don't hold the Parade on Sundays, so it fell to Monday, which is usually the holiday) I was up against three deadlines: First, preparing Sharon's script for her awards banquet presentation. Second, creating the certificates and compiling the awards that would be given in coordination with the script. And third, developing a PowerPoint presentation highlighting the photos of

Parade entries who were the award winners. This last one is important, because it's often the first time the Parade entries see what they look like in front of the crowd. I knew I could manage the first two tasks, but because of the looming deadline, lack of staff, and my vision issues, the third would be a challenge. The week before (as I had for months) I would come home and complain to Bill that there just weren't enough hours in the day to get everything done in a way that met my strict standards.

So, for this particular case he had an idea: He would sort through the thumbnail photos (which I had a difficult time seeing unless I made them large), find the best images, and drop them into the PowerPoint template according to the outline I created.

VA had installed some new restrictions on computer use, so I couldn't download the PowerPoint program on a thumb drive or email it to my personal email and do the work at home on my own time. Instead, I had to do it at work, and for Bill to help me, I'd have to log him on to a VA computer. To do that wasn't exactly in line with policy – he didn't have computer access clearance – but he was a registered VA volunteer and would not have access to any sensitive or confidential information. Besides, my former assistant, Anna Laurel, routinely logged on non-volunteers and told me it was a non-issue as long as they were supervised. The Phoenix VA Privacy Office, she said, confirmed this.

So, to ensure that I would not miss any deadlines, I logged Bill onto the computer to begin putting the images into the public presentation.

I didn't feel like any of this was "illegal" or underhanded. In fact, I did it right out in the open, in the director's lobby, where two computers were located along with couches and chairs for those waiting to go into the Director's suite. The Director's Office receptionist also had a desk there. We'd use the two computers for volunteers and occasionally new staff who needed a workstation until they could get theirs set. No big deal. But what I didn't realize was that someone was watching all this outside my office, someone who knew that Lance and Sharon had me in their sights. Someone who no doubt saw an opportunity to get in good with the new leadership by helping them go after a perceived threat to them. That someone was Dick Smith*, the Assistant Director of the medical center. As Dick later admitted, he knew Bill had helped me in the past, he was aware of my disability, and he had often seen my husband sitting next to me helping in "several situations" that involved the use of photos in my public affairs capacity.

In other words, what he'd seen could clearly be viewed as acceptable behavior that was consistent with past practices. Except Dick scampered off to Lance and reported that he had witnessed "suspicious" activity involving me, saying it seemed "strange" that Bill was logged onto a VA computer. Now, a reasonable person might sit back and think, "Hmm, it was okay then, but it's not okay now. What's wrong with this picture?"

But I knew, Lance wasn't reasonable, and the timing of what followed wasn't coincidental. When Dick squealed on me, Lance had to be happier than a kitten in a creamery.

On Dec. 4, he hauled me into his office and told me he had a statement from Dick about Bill being logged on to the computer. I didn't hesitate, admitting I'd done it. I went on to explain that Bill was helping me with the presentation, and that he was under my full supervision. I also asked him why this was a concern, reminding Lance that he knew full well Anna had often logged people on just as I had, and that as long as the Privacy Office was kept informed, it was considered an acceptable practice. To further support my case, I gave him the names of a number of people who could confirm Anna's log-on process (most of which he conveniently ignored down the road, as this story played out).

31

None of that mattered to Lance. On Dec. 5, VA security logged an "incident ticket" accusing me of a privacy and data breach.

The next day, Kim Tesh, one of the hospital's privacy officers, got a response. It stated:

> "PSETS0000083276 does not meet the criteria for a data breach and does not require any notifications." You may proceed with resolving the event and requesting the event closed."

She told Lance it didn't meet the "incident" threshold, but no one told me. In fact, I wouldn't find out it was determined a "no breach issue" for eight months when they had to provide the information under a Freedom of Information Act request.

Lance didn't care about the fact that I had been absolved or that I admitted to the error. He ignored the finding.

On Dec. 10, that ax that he seemed to be sharpening? It came down hard and fast.

7

LANCE MAKES HIS MOVE

On the morning of Dec. 10, I received a call from Lance asking me to meet with him at 2 p.m. I told him I'd be in the middle of a presentation to the hospital's leadership development staff but offered to come over right after.

No, he said. His request had become a demand: Be there precisely at 2 p.m. I was a little taken aback but then gave him what he (always) wanted: Yes, sir.

I still had to make my presentation. So, I went into the training session early, knowing I'd probably have to cut it short. I briefed the class on the hospital's public relations program, which had won a slew of national awards. I discussed how it had taken years to build our public relations program, our image and reputation, and I explained how we'd reached out to patients, volunteer staff, and Veterans Service Organizations for feedback on how we were doing. Then I shared how we used that feedback to improve. But it wasn't all rosy. I also talked to them about the present state of which the surveys showed declining employee morale and reputation. I then shared with them how they could help us rebuild our hospital and make it a workplace to be proud of.

As I was winding up to make my command performance for Lance on time, Shelby Roy* the Administrative Officer for Education Service, motioned to me from the back of the room, indicating it was time to leave. Walking back across the parking lot to see Lance, a feeling of anxiety settled over me like a dark cloud. I'm not sure why. Remember, Lance often summoned me, I'd show up, and he wouldn't be there. And if he was there, it would probably be another of his "floggings," which had become so frequent that I'd learned to steel myself against his abuse. That's not to say, though, that I ever got used to them or did not feel the sting.

So, despite the odd sense of apprehension, I really couldn't imagine how this would be different – just another humiliating encounter. Except it wasn't.

I knew something was up right away. When I checked in with Lance's secretary, I didn't get the usual "wait outside" or "it might be twenty minutes" or "he had a last-minute conflict." I was escorted into his office immediately. He wasn't alone. Maria Schmidt*, the Human Resources Director, was there, too. Alarms immediately started going off in my head.

Lance asked me to close the door then motioned me to a chair. There was a folder on his desk. He picked it up and pulled out a document.

"Paula," he began, his voice formal but still tinged with the kind of superiority only he could muster, "we're here today to discuss some allegations of misconduct that have been levied against you." *Misconduct?* I had no idea what he was talking about. "First, do you admit to logging your husband onto a VA computer on Nov. 29?"

There it was. The PowerPoint. I looked straight at him and didn't blink. "Yes."

He put that paper back in the folder and pulled out another. "And do you acknowledge that you know this is a violation of VA policy?"

"Yes." I also knew I'd supervised Bill, and Bill was a registered volunteer assigned to medical media, and what he did had more or less been standard operating procedure for some time. But it didn't seem like Lance was open to a debate, and I still didn't know exactly where this was headed.

He cleared his throat and took out a third document, pausing a moment, probably for effect. Or maybe it was to swallow his glee. "This is a memorandum from me to you. In it, I am involuntarily reassigning you out of your Public Affairs Officer position to the Education Department for thirty days while we investigate these serious allegations of misconduct against you."

Not just misconduct. *Serious allegations* of misconduct. My entire body went numb.

"We are removing you from your office during this time," he continued. "I will need your office key and your Blackberry. We will be removing your computer access, and we need you to sign this memorandum, acknowledging you received a copy of it."

I looked at it, dazed. One phrase leaped out: "An allegation of complaint was filed against you for possible misconduct. The misconduct alleged is of a very serious nature."

Somehow, I managed to break through the fog and think clearly. "I'm not able to sign anything right now. I need to talk to my employee representative."

Lance didn't like that, but there wasn't much else he could do. "Fine. I'll give you a copy of the memorandum. But during this time, you are not authorized to discuss this matter or this investigation with anyone. If anyone should contact you about any public affairs matters, you are to refer them to me. If there are any matters for follow-through on the Veterans Day Parade, you will also refer them to me. You are not to discuss anything about this with anyone."

He then gestured to the HR director, who had not said a word. "Maria will escort you to your office to gather your belongings. You are authorized to leave for the day." Then Maria led me out of the building.

Lance didn't specify what the accusations were, other than the allegation of "serious misconduct." He didn't say who had brought the complaint against me. He put a gag order on me. In other words, he denied me all the basic rights that are granted to any American in a similar situation. I didn't know the charges, could not face my accuser, and no longer enjoyed freedom of speech. It appeared as if Lance was playing the role of prosecutor and judge, and even set himself up as the person overseeing the investigation of my alleged infractions, which more or less made him my jury, too.

And let's not forget he was building his case on a "serious" allegation – Bill logging onto a computer – that just a few days earlier VA security had told him was an innocent policy violation, not a serious data breach, and that they, the privacy gurus, considered the matter closed. As I said previously, Lance omitted that little detail in coming down on me.

After I had been "escorted" from the building, I called Bill to come pick me up. By the time he got there, and I had a chance to tell him what was going on, the reality hit me. I was scared to death. My job and career were on the line, and I was being held hostage by a process Lance had created to get me out of his and Sharon's way.

I called my representative, Roger French, who lived in Loon Lake, Washington, an hour or so outside of Spokane, and recounted what had just happened. He was furious. He asked me to overnight Lance's memo to him, promising to review it, and he'd call me back the next day.

When he did, the news wasn't good.

8

YOUR ACTIONS ARE RETALITORY IN NATURE

I spent the first day of my "temporary assignment" lost and in tears. The world had come crashing down around me, hard, and I felt like I was at the whim of people whose only purpose in life was to destroy me. Worse, I didn't have the first idea of how this would end once Lance's 30-day investigation was over. But if past was prologue, as they say, it didn't look good.

Then there was the rumor mill, which was already in full swirl. A dear, dear friend of mine who was locked into the hospital's grapevine, called, wondering why I wasn't at work that day. I couldn't say anything or defend myself because of Lance's gag order. Roger, my representative, warned me that if I said one word, Lance would have a reason to fire me for insubordination. I could only stick to one mantra:

"I am not at liberty to say."

She said she'd heard I was taken out of my position for a privacy violation.

"I am not at liberty to say."

She asked if it was true that I was being investigated.

"I am not at liberty to say."

She said she needed some assistance on a project I typically did for her and wondered if there was anything I could do to help her.

"I am not at liberty to say."

She kept pressing, and I kept giving her the same answer. I'd known her for twenty years but couldn't tell her the truth. That would pretty much describe my life for the next eighteen months: Be quiet and do nothing while Lance, Sharon, and their yes-people appeared to be rallying to pursue my professional death by a thousand cuts.

In the insult-to-injury department, I also had to spend the morning going back and forth with Lance on the phone about my leave for the next few weeks. I had plenty of leave, and I needed to take a break., especially since I was now technically out of my job. With his trademark clipped, smugly official manner, he told me I'd have to work it out with Shelby Roy, the administrative officer for education who was also my new boss. That meant going into work, which at that point was about the last place I wanted to be.

Walking into the hospital, I knew there would be skeptical eyes and unspoken questions, but I had to see Shelby and had to give Lance a letter officially informing him that Roger would be representing me in this matter. So, I met with her and, strangely, our first stop was across the parking lot to my office on the sixth floor, which I'd been escorted out of the day before – and where I had been ordered not to return. She said we were there to "look at things." I couldn't help but wonder if this was some kind of set-up, a way for Lance to prove I'd disobeyed his orders and put me on the street. I didn't think Shelby was that kind of person. I knew Lance was.

After we'd "looked at things" – for whatever reason – I told her I needed to give Lance the letter. So, we waited to be buzzed into the director's office area, which housed the Pentad. (I know that sounds like a satanic nickname for the leadership, and I'll keep my thoughts on that to myself. But it really is what they were called – five leaders of the hospital, a Pentad.) Sharon Helman, the executive director, had the buzzer installed shortly after she arrived. It was a security lock on double doors, and the only way to get in was for someone to see you on the camera or through the glass door and buzz you in. Most of us thought it was a waste of money, but Sharon never seemed to miss an opportunity to send a message that she was more important than the rest of us little people.

Lance's secretary dutifully buzzed us in. I stood at his doorway and handed him the letter, which he took without a word. Then he went full bully again, hassling me over my leave requests and how they would be approved, making it all more complicated than it had to be. After he'd finished this ritual abuse-fest, Shelby and I left.

As we walked out, I tried to smile and nod at members of the Pentad's support staff, putting on a good front. I'd known many of them for some time, and our exchanges over the years had always been pleasant, but they kept their heads down and avoided eye contact, as if I no longer existed. I can only imagine Lance telling them about how I'd put the hospital, the patients, the employees, and the entire VA – hell, the entire country – in grave danger, and warning if they so much as glanced at me, their jobs would be on the line, too. Still, it kind of crushed me.

Our next stop was my office, again.

Shelby had me sit down and try to log on to my computer (or, rather, my previous computer) so she could get information on the projects I'd been working on. I tried to get into the system

40

three times, but it wouldn't take my password because I'd already been assigned another one for another computer. My suspicions came sneaking back. Lance had denied me access to this computer, but here was Shelby, trying to get me to sign on. It made no sense. The information she wanted was easily available to Lance through other avenues. It was also public affairs information, which he said I was to have nothing to do with.

Was this another ploy to show I violated his Dec. 10 memo? Was paranoia getting the better of me?

When this exercise in sign-on futility ended, I sent Roger a text. He told me to leave, concerned about any appearance of violating Lance's orders. Shelby and I left. We stopped on the first floor for a cup of coffee at a cart located in the middle of two large adjoining hallways. As we were talking, I saw several Phoenix VA employees looking at me with…what? Anger? Sympathy? Confusion? I couldn't tell, but I was rattled and suddenly realized that news of my "reassignment" had worked its way down from the sixth floor long before Lance had told me. I was the latest rumor on the mill but the last one, apparently, to hear about it.

I felt a wave of anxiety rolling in and knew I had to get out of there. Fast.

Telling Shelby I needed to call Roger, I went outside, passing more people who were hitting me with more odd looks. "I got the memo," he said after picking up the phone. "This is serious. Lance is coming after you criminally. We need to respond now."

I can't say it was a surprise, but hearing it from Roger, who was no novice at this kind of thing, hit me hard.

Shelby and I went to IT to pick up my new email and computer password for log on. Then we walked back across the parking lot to the Education Department where she asked me to sign in. Once I did, I checked my profile. It was blank. I looked in my email box, which typically contains hundreds of messages.

Empty. I looked on my calendar, expecting to see the usual three or four or five meetings per day. Nothing.

I didn't officially exist anymore on the computer. I was concerned that they were trying to erase me.

Although we'd never met, Roger French had represented me when Dr. Sam Foote and I first reported misconduct at the hospital in 2010. Roger is a retired VA human resources director with more than thirty-five years of federal service, and he knew the department's rules and regulations as if he'd written them himself. He was a tough negotiator and an even tougher advocate, the kind of guy who almost took it personally when the VA mistreated one of his clients. He'd also handled over forty cases against the department and knew how to win. He was someone the VA did not want to have knocking on its door.

That night, Roger and I worked on a draft of the response letter he wanted to send to Lance. It was brilliant, weaving his HR background, our prior experiences, my current relationship (such that it was) with the new leadership, and Lance's apparent bullying tactics into a single forceful document. He said all the right things, including raising the issue of why Shelby had asked me to log on to my old computer, calling it "highly irregular" given Lance's orders.

These two paragraphs followed (the reference to VISN 18 is the Veterans Integrated Services Network, which oversees medical centers in Arizona):

> "Further, and as you are aware, Ms. Pedene has had serious complaints against the medical center senior leadership during the past few years, which were not properly addressed by any of the existing leadership, including Mrs. Susan Bowers VISN 18 Network Director.

"Please understand that Ms. Pedene will highly suspect that your actions are retaliatory in nature. The fact that you have taken a very serious action, that you are unable to back up with appropriate evidence and/or including solid witness testimony, will further add to Ms. Pedene's suspicions and may result in significant litigation against yourself, Ms. Sharon Helman, Mrs. Susan Bowers, and the VA."

There it was. A warning shot. We were not going to go quietly.

9

FIND SOMETHING ON PAULA, AND QUICKLY

Lance knew (though I still didn't) that his "serious" allegations against me over the "privacy breach" were bogus, and Kim Tesh had received notification from VA security on Dec. 6 confirming that. So, he did the next best thing: He appealed it. While I don't presume nor want to read Lance's mind, I'm guessing he thought he needed to conjure up something else in case the data breach case fell apart. The appeal would give him time to do that and keep the heat on me while the higher-ups in D.C. were reviewing his request. Or, perhaps, he just wanted to pile it on, adding more charges in the hope that the "where there's smoke, there's fire" adage would play out.

On Saturday Dec. 8, he spoke with Janet Adams*, the hospital's Chief Financial Officer, and gave her a simple order: "Find something on Paula, and quickly."

Janet played along. She conducted a "random" audit of my public affairs spending. A random audit. Right. A one-year review might seem to be random, but instead, she went back ten years, looking at my purchases for products and services. Ten years of purchases that, by the way, had been approved through several layers of reviews and signed off on by contracting officers, former fiscal officers (including some who had been promoted to higher leadership positions in VA), the former Associate Director, and the director and his supervisors. That's not random. It's a fishing expedition, and it seemed to have only one purpose: to help Lance damage my career and force me out.

And you know what they caught? Minnows.

The exhaustive probe of my purchases revealed spending for pens, paper plates, cups, napkins, $120 in ads for the Veterans Day Parade, and $165 in blue ribbons for the Parade float winners. Not exactly budget-busting. What was also omitted from the finding was the fact that the purchase requests were submitted appropriately, approved by the previous leadership, and vetted through contracting. So, if I was guilty of mismanagement of funds, as they would later charge, why wasn't every person involved complicit in the conspiracy?

Of course, no one told me about any of this. I wouldn't learn of the fiscal audit until March of 2013, and only then it was from the churn of the rumor mill. Keeping me in the dark for as long as possible and letting the accusation pot simmer prevented me from providing any kind of aggressive response.

Despite not netting anything resembling a big fish, on Dec. 11, the day after Lance had removed me from my job, Janet sent him an email with the subject line "URGENT-Misuse of appropriated funds." It contained the following message:

> We have discovered the use of appropriated funds for the Veteran's Day Parade. This is in direct conflict with the guidance provided us. I do not feel these costs were necessary to our participation in the Parade.

So, I was now going to be persecuted for buying reams of colored paper that was necessary to notify the community of street closures as required by the City of Phoenix, a legitimate expense in support of the Parade that had been authorized by a long list of people up the ladder. Forget that it was, on the face, a silly, stupid, indefensible argument. Lance wanted to create a narrative that I was professionally corrupt, and he seemingly enlisted his colleagues and yes-people to spin whatever information he could find to fit that narrative. And to continue the absurd-on-its-face argument that this was all random, Lance responded to Janet's email by saying that maybe she shouldn't stop with my Fiscal 2012 spending, asking whether she believed "there may be misappropriation" in 2011 "that needed to be looked at as well." Janet had her marching orders.

It didn't stop there.

A few days after my "reassignment" meeting, Kim Tesh sent Lance an email saying that after reviewing other areas that may have been related to the "privacy breach," she had discovered photos of a hospital patient on the medical center's Facebook page. Naturally, she believed this was a new and additional privacy violation and argued that the "discovery" could lead to an additional amendment of the previous complaint that had been rejected and appealed; in other words, they thought they could reverse the previous determination by showing I was a serial data-breacher. The issue, she said, was that there was no form on file consenting to the public posting of the patient photo. Except there was. They just didn't look for it, nor did they ask me.

It was another example of how none of these people seemed to ever let the facts get in the way of a good character bashing. Here's what happened with the photo:

The staff in the hospital oncology ward had a patient who was in hospice care. They wanted to improve her spirits as best they could, so they created a "makeover day," giving her special personal care like a manicure and refreshed makeup. Photos were taken, and the family was happy. The nurses asked me about the process for getting the pictures posted on our social media sites. I gave them a consent form and told the nurse how she and the patient could fill it out.

Since the patient could not provide a complete signature, she marked it with an "X," and the nurse attached a note stating the patient's inability to sign and affirming that the "X" provided consent. The nurse also signed the form, and we filed it in the appropriate folder. The photos went online, and the staff and family thanked me for helping to share these dignified efforts at a difficult time for the patient and her family.

So, did we have consent? Yes, we did.

Was the patient's family upset about the photos? Nope, just the opposite.

Did Lance seem to care? Not even a little. Neither he nor Kim even asked if I'd gotten consent or where the form was – Kim even testified later there was no form on file. They just moved forward with yet another phony charge that appeared to support Lance's fictional narrative and could be used as "evidence" of yet another privacy breach by yours truly.

The revelation that I had posted a photo on Facebook gave my detractors another idea. Maybe my emails could reveal additional secrets. If so, monitoring them, without my knowledge, might provide even more examples of my "evil intentions".

On Dec. 20, the hospital's Chief Information Officer sent Lance an email saying they had secured permission for Shelby Roy to access my mailbox and review all of my email message traffic. Lance approved.

Big Brother, aka Lance Robinson, was now watching.

47

10
Holiday Cheerlessness

Being in the dark and knowing that something's going on that you can't see or understand is not easy. It really is like one of those horror movies where the character is trapped while unseen monsters circle for an attack. You feel scared and helpless, and it seems like there's no escape. All you can think about is how the monsters are going to break the door down, and what they're going to do to you and your family when they finally burst through.

That was me at Christmas.

When I first came to Phoenix, I had to cope with my vision issues. Just before my arrival, I'd been forced to stop driving because of them, and it was a shattering blow to my independence. On top of that, I was suffering from the constant shoulder pain that resulted from having to use a white cane to help me see. For years, I'd been fighting to stay positive (and largely succeeding) despite the fact that it always felt like more gloom was just around the corner. After the "reassignment" meeting with Lance, I turned

48

that corner and ran straight into a new nemesis: full-fledged depression.

Depression is an interesting thing. It comes and goes, it can last for months or even years, and it can disrupt every aspect of your life and daily activities. It causes emotional and physical pain. It triggers anxiety and fear. But bottom line, depression makes you feel sad and hopeless. Mixed with my history of being a workhorse and dealing with the reality that Lance seemed to be stealing my professional purpose, it made for a downer of a cocktail.

For the first time, I had to look at some serious medication for the depression. Initially, nothing seemed to work, and I had adverse reactions to several of the meds I was prescribed. I had heard about a Chinese herbalist, Dr. Judyth Shamosh. Her blend of "settle emotions" was designed to improve the flow of "qi" – vital energy – in my body and ease the heat around my heart and the stagnation in my liver that were brought on by depression. I was just trying to hang on, working with the herbalist and my psychologist to get through while Lance finished his 30-day investigation, and I could return to work. (My continued use of "30-day investigation" is no accident. You'll see why later.)

But back to Christmas.

As the holidays approached, I tried to stay cheerful in the face of a probe into my professional life whose direction and outcome were unknown. Although my siblings had noticed something was going on – how could they not? – only Bill knew the whole truth. He and I had discussed it and agreed that the time had come to let everyone else know the story.

Christmas dinner is a big deal in our family, which this year included seventeen people in all – our sons, my brothers and their wives, my sisters, their husbands, and nieces and nephews. We take turns hosting, and this year was mine. With my unexpected annual leave time, I had a chance to really plan the meal, figure out new ways to decorate the table, and decide how to reconfigure the furniture to make sure everyone could sit together and see each other. With that big a crowd, it was no easy task. For me, though, it was an added bit of needed therapy.

As we ate, however, my apprehensions started to bubble up. I got somber. My spirits began to drop. But what had to be done, had to be done.

"I have something I need to tell you," I said after we'd cleared the table, "and it's not going to be pleasant." You could almost feel everyone stop breathing. "I've been removed from my public affairs officer position at the VA hospital."

"Why?" my son Robert asked.

"They're saying I did something wrong, and my supervisor is investigating what they're calling serious misconduct allegations."

"Did you do it?" my other son, Steven, asked. "What they're saying?"

"Of course, she didn't," Bill replied, ever my knight and defender.

"What are they accusing you of doing?" Steven, again.

I thought about that for a second. You hate to keep anything from your kids, especially when you know that, at some point, it may influence them. But since I was already in hot water, I didn't want to say anything that might crank the temperature up even higher. Even here, in the privacy of my own home, in the presence of my own family, with people I knew I could trust with my life, I felt afraid to tell the whole truth.

"I'm a federal employee," I finally said. "And as a federal employee, I'm not at liberty to share too much. If I do, I could be charged with insubordination by my supervisor and be fired."

"But how will they ever find out?" Steven asked.

I didn't want to sound paranoid and say, because they find out everything. Investigations can go anywhere, however, and you never know what or how something will find its way into the official record. "I'm sorry. I just think it's best for all of us if I don't say anything more."

For a moment or two, everyone just sat there in a stupor of disbelief. Then they started peppering me with question after question, and legitimately so. All I could do was deflect with my non-answer answers.

I had dreaded this moment.

Bill and the boys had been through the Reyes and Beam incident, and they saw that at times, it had been tough on me. Similarly, I saw that it had been tough on them. Looking at Steven and Robert, I could almost see it in their eyes: Is what happened before going to happen again? The last thing I wanted to do was visit (or revisit) my workplace issues on them. Robert had just started going to community college and was doing well. Although he was still dealing with some emotional struggles, Steven was finishing his senior year in high school and had just been accepted into the Comedy Club and Humanities track, which included theatre, and he excelled at both.

And now, I was risking throwing both of them into a tailspin for reasons I didn't fully know and couldn't explain even if I did.

I could see Robert's anger starting to rise. He's a sensitive boy, quiet, tall, slender, blond haired and blue eyed. It took a lot to make him mad. "I don't understand why this is happening," he said.

I tiptoed out on a limb. "There are some people at the hospital who are afraid I might do or say something to hurt them."

"Like what? What did you do to them?" Steven asked.

I smiled weakly. "That's the strange part. I haven't done anything."

"Then why?"

"I don't know. I guess because they can."

"Don't they see all you've done, how hard you work, how good you are at your job?" Robert said. "Doesn't any of that matter?" I shook my head slowly. "So, what's going to happen now?"

"It will be a process," I said. "Supposedly thirty days. But it could be longer, and if it is, it might get hostile and expensive. We may have to hire lawyers to fight back."

Robert and Steven looked at each other, then at me. When Steven asked, "Are we going to have to sell the house?" I almost came apart.

Finally, my middle brother Frank piped up. "Paula, you're going to come out of this okay. Even though it sounds bad and seems challenging, you're going to get through it."

I flashed another weak smile. "I hope so." He asked if there was anything they could do. "Just say your prayers for me."

Little did I know, given that 2013 was going to be anything but a happy new year, how badly I'd need those prayers.

11

A ROADMAP TO CONSPIRACY

For the Record...

On April 26, 2010, William Schoenhard, the VA Deputy Undersecretary for Health Administrative Operations, wrote a memo to the directors of the Veterans Integrated Service Network, or VISN, that said, "It has come to my attention that in order to improve scores on assorted access measures, certain facilities have adopted inappropriate scheduling practices sometimes referred to 'gaming strategies.'" He went on to attach a list of these practices – there were about two dozen of them – that VA facilities across the country were using to reduce the official recorded wait times for patients seeking care.

Two of them stand out.

The first discussed the use of a "logbook or other manual system, for scheduling patient appointments." Mr. Schoenhard wrote, "Using this method, appointments are scheduled in VistA at a later date instead of placing patients on the EWL." To explain: VistA was a somewhat ancient patient scheduling program that had been around for about twenty-five years; EWL stands for "electronic waiting list," which is the official record of when a patient called in and when his or her appointment was actually scheduled. To translate, he was saying that a written appointment logbook could be used to prevent long wait times from being entered onto the EWL. In other words, the date a patient called to schedule an appointment – which would be entered into the written logbook – would not correspond to the date on the EWL, which would be entered later. Thus, it would look like the wait times for veterans seeking care were shorter than they actually were.

The second tactic involved "desired dates" of patient appointments. Here's how NBC News described it in a May 13, 2014 report:

> The date the patient wants to see a doctor is supposed to be entered as the "Desired Date," but those dates are often sooner than a doctor is available. Facilities were able to hide the difference between what the patient wanted and what the patient got, according to the memo, by either entering the wrong date, neglecting to enter any date or entering the earliest available date as the patient's desired date.
>
> The memo reveals that some clerks look inside the electronic scheduling system to see what dates are actually available before filling in the "Desired Date. The clerk [finds] the availability of future appointments. Once a date/time is found, the clerk exits the system and then starts over, using the identified date/time as the Desired Date."

Why does this matter?

VA facilities are rated in part by how quickly they provide veterans access to care. Hospital executives get their bonuses, based in part, by how quickly their facilities do that. So, if the official records show that patients are being scheduled within, say, two weeks of their initial call – rather than the actual six or seven months – the facilities could then improve their standing within VA, and the executives could make more money in performance bonuses. Of course, veterans suffer, but for some, that seems to be a secondary consideration.

Mr. Schoenhard's intentions were good. His goal was to ensure accuracy in scheduling and end what he diplomatically called "workarounds" in the process. "Our expectations," he wrote, "are that there will be no workarounds, and that access will continue to improve with integrity and honesty in all the work we do."

The problem was, not all of the administrators were poster children for integrity and honesty, and rather than eliminating these questionable practices by pointing them out, Mr. Schoenhard had unwittingly given every hospital executive a roadmap for manipulating the system for their own gain.

12

TRAPPED IN AN INSTITUTIONAL HELL

B y January, the holidays had come and gone, but the petty indignities didn't stop. If I had any hope that the close of Lance's 30-day investigation would wind down some of the harassment, I was sorely mistaken.

Shelby Roy, who I thought had some empathy for what was happening to me, suddenly seemed as if she'd pitched a tent in the Lance camp. She asked me if I wanted to move out of the cramped office we shared and into the library on the third floor. I gladly agreed, looking forward to the opportunity to interact with people. But on my second day there, she came over to "check on me." (I guess taking a previously unoccupied desk at the front of the library was a matter of grave concern.) Once there, she began to chastise me for any infraction she found in my job performance. I found that odd given that I didn't have a whole lot of responsibility except helping patients locate the information they needed and assisting physicians with their searches for medical journals and research articles. I mean, what's to find fault with in any of that? But she did, no doubt under Lance's orders to make my life miserable.

It was day after day of little stuff:

Shelby sent me a note demanding that I change my title on the hospital computer from Public Affairs Officer to Education Technician – a somewhat formal reminder of my "fall."

I asked for the special ergonomic chair I had in my office on the sixth floor, and for my Day Timer and snail mail. Stu Jones*, who Sharon had designated as the acting public affairs officer, came down to the library with the Day Timer but not much else. When he walked in and saw me, he had this big grin on his face. "Who's this new employee in the library?" he said. No one laughed. Funny guy. I asked if the rest of the things I'd requested were coming. "I've only got two hands, Paula," he replied. That was the end of that.

Then I got a note from Shelby: "Paula, the library has ergonomic chairs already in place, so unless you have a physician's note for the chair from your office, you'll have to make do." I responded by sending her documentation from a VA safety specialist who had recommended that I get the special chair, which helped me sit directly in front of the computer to enhance my line of sight. My response went nowhere.

I looked up my name in the hospital directory. It was blank. I called Roger and told him of Shelby's request. We decided to list my title as Temporary Education Technician. That way, people knew it was temporary. Still, the title change (which came from Shelby) was unethical. It didn't fit my job description, nor did it reflect the federal position I was legally appointed to. But to my browbeaters, it was just another way to try to put me in my place.

Meanwhile, the rumor mill was shifting into overdrive.

A patient told Mark Simmons, the library team lead who is a wonderful man with a beautiful Christian spirit, that the "new

PAO" Stu Jones said he'd been moved to the sixth floor "because the female public affairs gal who used to work there messed up badly, and he isn't sure if she's going to be able to get her job back."

That didn't surprise me coming from Stu. I sensed he didn't like the fact that I was a grade above him. He also took a page out of Lance's playbook, asking me more than once when I was going to retire. The first two times, I laughed it off. The third time, I confronted him, noting he'd raised the same question twice before. "So, what would you do differently as the public affairs officer?"

He replied, "It's what I wouldn't do."

It appeared to me that his vision of the public affairs program would be reshaped to serve the needs of the leadership, not the patients nor the staff. It wasn't long before the free flow of information among patients, staff, and community dried up. (Although Stu was less concerned about the flow of private information about me – the gal who "messed up badly.")

Meanwhile, the rumors that I had engaged in a massive privacy violation started growing louder, despite the fact that Lance and Kim Tesh (but not me) both knew they were false. Then the charge that I was being investigated for inappropriate expenditures of medical center funds started circulating. Once again, there was no truth to that because Lance and Janet knew the spending had been approved and vetted according to hospital guidelines. But I couldn't defend myself because Lance had put me on a gag order about the "investigation," so I had no recourse but to stay silent while the gossip and hearsay swirled around me.

I was trapped in an institutional hell, where lies were becoming truth because management was abusing its right to investigate and prevent the falsehoods from being exposed for what they were.

I just kept telling myself, *keep your head down, keep your head down. This, too, shall pass, and by the end of the 30-day investigation when the facts are clear, good will win out.*

Boy was I wrong. On every account.

13

PARANOIA STRIKES DEEP

I don't want to sound like a broken record, but when "they" are coming after you, and you know who "they" are and that "they" will stop at nothing to get you, there's a tendency to get a little paranoid. Every little thing, innocent or not takes on a larger, darker meaning. You don't trust people. You're suspicious of everyone and their motives. You can't shake the feeling that the world is hell-bent on hurting you.

It's not a great place to be. But it's what I was slipping into.

For example, when I was first banished to the library, one of my responsibilities was to help patients create an account on MyHealtheVet, a program that allowed them to interact with their providers over a secure email message system. It also offered some added benefits that could only be accessed through a two-step verification process, which involved taking their Social Security numbers and other personal information and sending it to the Release of Information Office for vetting. But because Lance had determined I was a "security threat," that part of the process was off limits to me.

After a few weeks in the library, Mark Simmons – the library lead and, as I said, a truly good man – decided to allow me to help register patients into the MyHealtheVet system. All he needed was Shelby Roy's approval. Surprisingly, she agreed.

My paranoia alarms went off. Here I was, someone who had supposedly "messed up bad," a person whose character and integrity were being questioned at every turn, who was under review for a "massive security breach or violation" and accused of "mismanagement of funds," and I was suddenly being allowed to handle personal, confidential materials from our nation's veterans? I had the patients' SSNs, I helped them create passwords, I could see their emails – which meant I could view their personal data any time I wanted.

It made no sense.

Was Mark, a dear friend, collaborating with the leadership?

Was Shelby helping Lance prepare a case against me?

Was I being lured into a trap so they could fire me?

I called Roger. "It is concerning," he said.

"Are they trying to set me up?"

"I don't know. But they're asking you to do this as part of your regular duties, so I'm not sure you have much choice. Do what they say. I don't like it, but they can add or take away your responsibilities as they see fit." There's an understatement, I thought. "Just stay sharp and never let your guard down."

Easier said than done.

I was also becoming obsessed with the Medical Center's attempts to make me disappear. I sent out an email on an upcoming medical education event and discovered that my message came from "no name." I started rifling through all the various hospital telephone directories for my name listing, but it wasn't there. Same with emails. Patients and staff who came to the library said they were surprised I was there; trying to find me on the sixth floor, they'd been told I no longer worked at the hospital. Anyone calling my work number got the same message. Meanwhile, Lance was strutting around the building saying, "Paula is never coming back" to anyone who would listen.

So, forgive me if I was starting to see conspiracies around every corner.

One Saturday, I got a call from Jean Simpson*, the public affairs officer from the Veterans Integrated Service Network. I'd worked with her for years, and we'd created a bond – or so I thought. She was aware of the mess in Phoenix and how my relationship with Lance was steadily eroding. I knew that the removal of a high-profile public affairs person was something folks inside of the VA needed to know and that it would eventually work its way up the chain. Jean was good enough to give me an update as to where Lance's investigation was so far.

"It should be close to complete," she said, "because it's coming up on your thirty days."

"Except it's been more than thirty days."

She paused. "Have you heard anything?"

"Nothing."

Was she fishing just to see what I knew? She shifted subjects.

"What are you doing in your detail?" she asked.

More fishing? Trying to get confirmation I had access to confidential information? "It's pretty mundane. Checking books in and out. Getting approvals for continuing medical education. That kind of thing."

Then she shifted back to my current troubles. "Why don't you have your representative call and ask what's up with the investigation?"

Did she know something I didn't know and wasn't telling me?

"Maybe I will," I replied. Then I took a deep breath and found the courage to ask the question that kept me up at night and was at the heart of everything: "What do you think all this is going to do to my career at VA and my future as a public relations professional? Do you have any job opportunities at VISN?"

"Paula, before we go into that, you need to get through this investigation. Clear your name. Work with them and do what they say until you find other employment."

Other employment? "What would you do if you were me?"

"Honestly, I'd start looking for work outside of VA."

She had to know something. It was the same refrain I'd been hearing from Lance and Stu Jones – get out, retire, go somewhere else, anywhere but here. Had someone issued talking points? Was Jean, a friend, colleague, and confidante, part of this investigation, too?

"They're trying to wear you down," she said before hanging up. "Don't let them."

I'll admit, this was my mind over-reaching. Jean and Mark weren't my enemies. They weren't Lance. They weren't trying to take me down. They had little to gain if I fell. Maybe I just needed to take a step back and get out of my own head. Maybe this would all sort itself out.

Then I got a call. Any hope that I was in some way a victim of my own imagination was about to go right out the window.

On the day the call came, the strangest thing happened.

A patient who was a regular in the library and who only knew me there, told me she had a meeting with Stu Jones. She wanted to discuss the possibility of a friend doing some videotaping at the hospital and needed Stu's okay since he was the "acting public affairs officer." While visiting him in my former office, she noticed some photos on the desk. Not of his wife, kids, or parents. Not of some fishing trip or camping expedition.

They were pictures of me and my family. "Why do you have pictures of Paula in here?" she asked.

"Oh, that's not Paula," he said. "That's Ginger, another employee. She's in charge of contracts, and that's who you need to talk to about your video request, not me."

(Memo to Stu: Lying is generally frowned upon in the PR business.)

The patient was a bit confused, so she came down to the library, told me about the photo, and asked if it was indeed me. I told her it was, and as proof gave her a business card with my picture and personal information on it, something I had created at day forty of my 30-day investigation after seeing how the hospital was trying to delete my existence.

She looked at the card and then up at me. "Why would he say that?"

What I could have said was that providing false and misleading information and operating under a "lack of candor" or truthfulness was an infraction that warranted personnel action, or at least it would someplace where leadership didn't have the integrity of a rattlesnake. So, I simply replied with a variation of I am not at liberty to say. "It's a long story."

Good Lord, I was thinking, sitting back down at my desk. Who are these people?

The phone rang. It was someone I knew and trusted. "Paula, I need to tell you something."

I hesitated. "Okay."

"The Criminal Division of the Office of the Inspector General has opened an investigation of you."

Criminal? My voice dropped to a near whisper, and I kind of leaned my head into my shoulder, like I was worried about prying eyes and lip readers. "What? Why?"

"They are looking at your use of funds from your VA budget and your contractors."

I could hardly breathe. "I don't understand."

"They say there's the appearance of misuse of funds and inappropriate expenditures."

Impossible, I thought. Everything I'd done, everything I'd ever done, was according to the books.

I was too shaken to ask anything else. Besides, the library was not the place for it. So, I hung up, got myself together as best I could, and went outside, shaking and crying.

That night, I called Roger with the news. "You need a criminal lawyer," he said. I started crying again, sobbing so hard the words would not come. "Paula, you need to listen to me," he continued sternly. "This is what they're counting on. You coming apart. It's how they win. The only way you can beat this thing is to fight back. Can you do that?"

"Yes," I managed.

"Do you know a criminal attorney?"

"No."

"Do you know where you can find one?"

I didn't, but I promised I would look. I had no idea he'd come to me by way of Vietnam.

14

I HAVE NEVER SEEN THE HOSTILITY

After Roger's bombshell of a recommendation to hire an attorney, I started thinking about criminal lawyers. Given the situation and the players, my focus was on veterans I knew who could either do the job or point me in the direction of someone who could. One name came to mind:

Rick Romley, the former Maricopa County Attorney and Marine Corps veteran who lost both legs to a mine explosion in Vietnam in 1969.

I had served with Rick on a nonprofit board, had him come and speak at the hospital about his time in Southeast Asia, and had watched him as he artfully handled difficult case after difficult case as county attorney. When I told him what was happening to me, he was intrigued. Although he said he wanted to help, he had too many other clients at the time that were working on VA contracts. So instead, he suggested that I contact someone else, another veteran who was now a criminal attorney:

Joe Abodeely.

During the war in Vietnam, Joe served with the Army 1ˢᵗ Air Cavalry. He was something of a hero, as the Los Angeles *Herald Examiner* reported:

> A two-mile victorious march by the Army 1st Air Cavalry Division formally ended the 78-day Communist siege of the fort Hanoi vowed it would take and American generals pledged would never be lost. The siege was over but the battle for control of South Vietnam's Communist-infested northern frontier roared on…
>
> At Khe Sanh, where round the clock Communist artillery fire had driven 6000 Marine defenders underground, the Leathernecks Sunday whooped it up as Army 1st Lt. Joe Abodeely's unit walked the last two miles into the camp. Abodeely, 24 of Tucson, Ariz. and his platoon formed the 1st Air Cavalry spearhead of the 20,000-man Operation Pegasus drive that broke the Communist grip around Khe Sanh in a week-long drive that covered 12 miles of jungle, hills and minefields…

Reading between those lines, it was clear to me that Joe was someone who never backed down and never shied away from fighting the good fight. In other words, the kind of lawyer I needed.

I didn't know him, except by reputation. He'd become a successful defense attorney in Phoenix after leaving the Army and was known to be one tough son of a bitch. I was a bit intimidated at the thought of meeting him, let alone asking him to represent me, but I figured that to fight an SOB (that would be Lance), you needed an SOB. So, we got together at the Arizona Military

Museum where he was volunteering, and I explained what was happening and why I needed a criminal attorney. He took the case on the spot. I paid his upfront fee (borrowed from my life insurance account) and arranged for a call between him and Roger to begin their collaboration.

I wasn't quite sure what to expect when the two of them teamed up. As I'd come to know Roger better, there was no doubt in my mind that he was tough, too, though in kind of an understated way. Imagine a Navy Seal who spoke with a quiet reserve, like a college professor with a killer instinct. Joe, on the other hand, was everything his military career implied: a stop-at-nothing, larger-than-life warrior whose colorful language could curl a sailor's hair. Put the two of them in the same room and get ready for fireworks.

In February, almost sixty days into Lance's "30-day investigation," Roger told me he'd had enough of the hospital's BS and how I was being treated. He said he'd talked with Joe, and they had worked up a letter to Veterans Affairs Secretary Eric Shinseki, signed by Roger. It opened by recounting the issues that led to the departures of Reyes and Beam and rightfully praised the VA for identifying mismanagement and improving the overall environment for staff and patients after they were gone.

Then the fireworks started.

The letter blasted Lance and Sharon, saying that with their hiring, "progress of providing quality patient care, maintaining employee morale and community support have again started to decline." It noted that Sharon had hired her husband, despite laws, rules, and regulations prohibiting that sort of nepotism; harshly criticized her handling of Equal Employment Opportunity cases; and charged that Lance had lowered the performance rating of a female employee after she told Sharon she feared he was going to hit her.

Next, they got to me. The language was blistering:

- I had been "humiliated, made fun of, encouraged to retire, and ridiculed and discriminated against based on gender and disability," and Lance was harassing me with Sharon's "tacit approval."
- When I questioned Lance about my staff and budget cuts, "he threw a temper tantrum" that had me fearing he was going to "physically assault" me.
- Lance was conducting a "systematic 'witch hunt' to find issues" with my performance and conduct.
- After sixty days, I still had not been informed about what I'd allegedly done wrong, nor had I been charged with any wrongdoing.
- I had been told that I could not talk to anyone other than my representative, but Lance and Stu Jones had "released information to others within the Medical Center and to other medical centers."
- On the rights that I'd been denied: "Where is due process in this instance, specifically, the right to know you're being investigated, and when did responsible management officials notify the employee of her right to representation?"

Then came the kicker:

"I have donated my assistance to forty employees in the VA system nationwide. Most of my consultations have been with the employees at the VA Medical Center in Phoenix. I must tell you after thirty-three years as a Personnel Officer with the VA… I have never seen the hostility, cavalier violations of regulations and laws, nor have I seen the total lack of common sense in a single facility as I have observed at the VAMC Phoenix, AZ."

When Roger read the letter to me, I didn't have a single edit. It went out to VA Secretary Shinseki.

Meanwhile, Joe sent another letter to the VA Regional Counsel in Phoenix asking about the status of Lance's "30-day investigation." He was told it was "ongoing." Another non-response response. Never being one to acknowledge defeat, Joe called the VA lawyers to press them on the case and got pretty much nothing. It was becoming obvious, to him at least, that they just did not care about what was going on in Phoenix or what leadership was doing to me. That night when we spoke on the phone, he started raging about how VA was infringing on my rights and how stupidly this was all being handled. I was so depressed, all I could do was listen and make my points when he stopped to take a breath, wondering through my growing haze of depression if and when the letter to Secretary Shinseki would somehow deliver me from this darkness.

It didn't. But while there may have been a lack of action in D.C., Lance and his collaborators had no intention of hitting pause.

15

FIGHT THEM

As the "30-day investigation" hit the 90-day mark, the mind games continued. Some of it was the usual petty nonsense. For example, I found out that my name, photos, and anything else related to me had been stripped from the *Desert Sun*, the Phoenix VA's bi-monthly newsletter that I wrote for and edited for eighteen years. It was a slap in the face. I felt as if someone (can't imagine who) had already decided I was guilty of a crime and had handed down a sentence before I even knew what the charge was, who brought it, or had a chance to defend myself.

I'll say it again: This probably sounds like nothing more than a series of minor annoyances, but I'd been enduring them every day for months, and over time, minor things add up to major things, and they take a toll. My depression got deeper.

Then my accusers pulled out the big gun.

I received a call from Katherine Brooks, a high school classmate of mine who had been serving on the board of Honoring Arizona's Veterans, which funded the Phoenix

Veterans Day Parade. "I just spoke with Sharon Helman," she said. At this point in leadership's campaign against me, that was not a discussions starter I was eager to hear. "She's got some concerns."

"About what?" I asked.

"About us moving forward with the VA with the Parade." She paused. "And she said you wouldn't be available to help, either."

I was furious and crushed at once. "They can't just pull out of the Parade."

"She thinks they can coordinate the event themselves, without you and without us."

That was crazy. The Parade had more than 100 entries, attracted 45,000 spectators, and generated millions of positive media impressions. I started it in 1997, and with all humility, I had it running like a well-oiled machine. And now Sharon, out of nowhere with nothing but pure spite, wanted to throw a monkey wrench into the works? She was fully aware how important the Parade was to me. She also had to know that because of the Parade, we had not only dramatically improved the community's perception of the Phoenix VA but had also increased the number of veterans who turned to the hospital for treatment. That's not an idle boast, either. We had research to prove it. But she didn't care.

Katherine gently pressed me about what was going on. I could only tell her there was an investigation, and that I'd hired an employee representative and a lawyer to help me fight it. "Lance has prohibited me from saying anything and told me I can't have any involvement in the Parade," I said. "So unfortunately, I can't help you."

That didn't make Katherine happy. "Well, we'll see about that."

A few days later, I got another call, this one from Stan Skorniak, who I'd worked with for ten years in Phoenix. He had been an up-and-comer in the VA system and was, at this time, the No. 2 at the John J. Pershing Medical Center in Poplar Bluff, Missouri. I had always been a fan of Stan's and supported his rise at several turns. In a world where my personal network had dwindled from thousands to a few dozen, I knew he was one of the few people I could count on.

Stan had heard what was going on with me. I couldn't tell him much, just the basics – like what I'd said to Katherine. He offered to talk to Human Resources on my behalf and check back with anything he found.

What he learned was not especially positive: Lance had the authority to keep me under investigation for up to a year, and there was nothing I could do about it. While I had already concluded that the "30-day investigation" was a nicely dressed lie, this confirmed it. Lance had the right to bludgeon me for twelve months. I had no rights at all.

That didn't mean I had to take it sitting down. But in fact, I did.

At my computer.

With Google as my co-pilot.

I am not a vengeful or angry person by nature. Those emotions don't live in my heart, and they fly in the face of my Christian beliefs and values. But I am not going to sugar coat it. After Katherine's call about the Parade and the knowledge that Lance could torment me for far longer than thirty days, I was not happy. So, I did about the only thing I felt I could. I went online and Googled Sharon Helman. I didn't know exactly what I was looking for or what I'd find, but it didn't matter. I had been treading water for months, going nowhere. Doing research would at least feel like progress. At the very least, maybe I'd see something that boosted my morale.

One of the first articles I found was in the Jan. 8, 2010 edition of the *Spokane Spokesman-Review* that was published around the time Sharon was scheduled to leave the Medical Center there and take over the Hines, Ill. VA Hospital. It was hardly a morale booster – at least for anyone but Sharon. It read like a paid advertisement.

The article praised her for the "admirable job" she did in Spokane and for winning "bipartisan praise and confidence from Republican Congresswoman Cathy McMorris Rogers and Democratic Sen. Patty Murray." It further quoted Murray as saying it would be difficult for Spokane to find a replacement with Sharon's "'unparalleled' skills at problem-solving and communication."

Problem-solving and communication skills? Give me a break.

I was sort of deflated but shared the article with Roger anyway. He called me back fast.

"I'm curious," he said. "Did you look at the comments under the story?" I told him I hadn't. "There are three of them you might find interesting. Read them and get back to me."

I did. Pay dirt.

Comment No. 1: "Who wrote your editorial on Sharon Helman? Was it anyone who knew her? Did you talk to any of the patients or staff at the facility? Obviously not. You painted such a rosy picture of her abilities, however, you neglected to talk about the gargantuan swath of destruction she has levied on three VA facilities: Roseburg, Walla Walla, and Spokane! Ask the staff and patients of these facilities. Most are hosting 'Good Riddance' parties after she left, we were so glad to see her go. She and her mentor Max Lewis displayed their disdain of the needs of the patients and those who provided the hands-on care by cutting staff to bare bones levels and never asking those at the grass roots for their opinions of programs and expenditures. Everything was about image, and it seems our VISN leaders, legislators, and the local media bought it hook, line and sinker. Thank God, she is gone…"

Comment No. 2: "As an employee of the Spokane VAMC for over twenty years, I was amazed how off base the editorial was. The editorial sounded like it was written by the public affairs officer of the Spokane VA, who was hired by Sharon Helman… If anyone took the time to look at the path of destruction she left from her position of Associate Director at Roseburg VAMC and then her year as Director at the Walla Walla VA, and then Spokane, they would find unhappy veterans, massive upheavals of good employees, dissatisfied employees, beaten down service chiefs, and ultimately no better care for the Vets…We at the Spokane VAMC are celebrating her departure."

Comment No. 3: "Ask the Vets and they will tell you that Helman was just more lip service and smoke. She kept the VA fax numbers secret because so many Vets were faxing in complaints. Her speech last year at Veterans Day (2008) was hollow, uninspiring, and filled with untruthful promises."

Swath of destruction. Path of destruction. Celebrating her departure. Good riddance parties. Untruthful promises.

Wow.

I had to wonder how in the world Sharon had risen in the ranks while breeding that kind of hostility. We had all heard rumors that she was politically savvy, well connected, and knew how to play the game like a pro. But if even a fraction of what was said in those comments was true, we had all seriously underestimated her.

During my conversation with Stan Skorniak, he suggested I reach out to Glenn Costie. Glenn and I went back to 2004, when we were both in the Leadership VA class, so I knew him well and admired him. He'd worked his way up the ladder from Engineering Chief to Director of the Poplar Bluff Center and ethically earned every promotion he received.

I'd called him before about the "investigation," and this time he got back to me. I couldn't tell him much about what was happening – again, just the broad strokes – but we did agree that if I could provide him a non-specific "scenario," he could offer some advice on how one might deal with that given situation.

So, I painted a generic picture for him: An employee is put into a detail outside his or her official position while undergoing an investigation from the Administrative Investigative Board and/or the Office of Inspector General Criminal Division. The individual in question is unaware of the status of the investigations. He or she is simply sitting and waiting.

Glenn is no fool. I didn't have to spell it out for him. He understood exactly what I was saying without me saying it. He gave me what sounded like a warning: "Sharon has a serious level of protection somewhere high up in the organization. People say she's emotionally based and not objective."

Was he telling me to be careful? To back off?

Hardly.

"You should fight them," he said. "What they're doing to you doesn't sound right. You've done stellar work in Phoenix, and you can't let them take that away from you."

Meanwhile, back at the library, I was trying to do the best job I could under the circumstances, but the circumstances were starting to weigh heavily on me, and the humiliations continued.

Lance wasn't acting on my leave requests because, I was told, he didn't have to approve them in a timely fashion. One day, I removed a large stack of blank copy paper that was cluttering up a desk and got chewed out for it by another member of the staff,

Ray Small* — someone who, I later learned, was funneling negative information about me to Shelby Roy and, presumably, to Lance. When I tried to help a patient with My HealtheVet, Ray told me I was not to assist with the request and should send the veteran someplace else to get it done. I asked if that was the best customer service, ignoring their needs and pushing them out the door. He jumped all over me, saying my comment degraded him.

I didn't get the right assistance either with a previous job injury I reported after falling down a flight of stairs and suffering a small fracture in my pelvic bone. At the time, Dick Smith seemed to be violating federal guidelines that required management to assist in completing and sending my worker's compensation form to the appropriate office. He just refused to do it, leaving me to wallow in process limbo. I eventually had to fill out the form myself with the help of others. There was no reason for Dick's refusal.

With the day-to-day indignities and humiliations, it felt like the world was piling on. Little by little, the joy was draining out of my soul, replaced by a deep sadness. I was having regular appointments with my therapist by this time, trying to see my way through a situation I had no control over, one with no end in sight. My evenings were spent in discussions with Roger or Joe, crying, the phone in one hand, a wine glass in the other. The pressure was becoming unbearable, and I was beginning to wonder if I'd ever be able to climb out of this hole that Lance and Sharon had dug for me.

Then, unexpectedly, I got a shovel.

16

AT LAST, A VICTORY

It was a quiet day in the library, and I was sitting at my desk, enduring my new routine when Joe called. "Can you talk?" he asked.

"Sure."

"Dennis Wagner just called me." I bolted out of the chair and went into the hallway, motioning to Mark Simmons that it was my lawyer, and I needed to speak with him outside the workspace.

This was either very good news or very bad news. Dennis was an extremely competent and well-respected investigative reporter with the *Arizona Republic*. I knew Dennis. He's a tough but fair journalist, and as the hospital's public affairs officer, I'd gone to great lengths to make sure the VA wasn't on his radar in a negative way. My rule talking with him was simple: Listen carefully, only answer what he asked, and keep it short and to the point. If you were in his crosshairs, the last thing you wanted to see over your morning cup of coffee was a Dennis Wagner byline.

Joe relayed bits and pieces of their conversation without being especially forthcoming, finally saying, "If he calls you directly, you are not to respond." Of course, I knew that, thanks to Lance's gag order.

"I understand. But what is he working on?"

"I'll tell you tomorrow. In the meantime, do you have any photos of yourself working on the Parade and helping veterans?"

Only about a thousand, I thought. I gave him links to pictures from the 2012 Parade. He thanked me without any further explanation and hung up.

I was a wreck the rest of the day. I respected Dennis but had no idea where he would take this. My head played no-win situations over and over. Was I about to get caught in a media ambush? Had Lance fed him the leadership's line about the data breaches and financial mismanagement charges? Was Joe playing defense to divert a PR nightmare? And what if the story put me in a good or sympathetic light? Would Lance use it as a weapon and come at me with more false accusations, saying publication was proof that I'd violated the gag order, and use that to fire me?

All I could think of was a quote I'd once heard: Be careful that your worst enemy isn't the one between your ears. Nice thought, but not too terribly comforting at this moment.

The next day, March 28, Roger called, telling me he and Joe had been working with Dennis on a piece for the *Republic*. "It's about you," he said. "About how you were removed and how the hospital isn't handling your investigation according to VA regulations."

I was stunned and more than a little scared. If the story took that angle, Sharon and Lance would be furious.

"Talk to Joe," he continued, "but do it after work."

Waiting has never been a strength of mine. "Can't I just go out into the hallway and call him, or outside the building?"

"No."

"Why not?"

"Because there are eavesdroppers everywhere."

Lance did have his little network of yes-men and spies, his own personal NSA.

"Oh," he added, "one more thing." His voice was somewhere between ominous and warning. "The story is supposed to break tomorrow. Be ready for a rough day at work."

A rough day at work. Like there was any other kind.

I got home as quickly as I could and called Joe.

"I'm disgusted with this case, Paula," he said, "all of it. What they're doing to you, how they're doing it. The VA still isn't responding to me. Nobody's telling us what we have every right to know. So, when Dennis got a tip about what was happening, and found out I was your lawyer, he called me."

Ever the follow-the-rules girl, I asked, "Did he talk to VA to get their side of the story?"

"He submitted a query to the hospital. No response."

Not to go all sour grapes, but no response is a bad strategy. If it were me, I'd have said, tell the truth and get ahead of the story as quickly as you can. That's smart PR. But I wasn't making the call. Sharon and Lance were. They were the organ grinders, and Stu was the monkey. With that trio, truth never stood a chance.

"Roger and I talked," Joe added, "and we decided the hell with it, let's give Dennis the story."

I'm not an early riser, but the next morning I was up and out of bed at dawn. Bill, in typical fashion, was already in the kitchen, making coffee like he usually does, doing whatever he could to get me out the door – which was becoming tougher and tougher these days. He's such a jewel. On more than one occasion, I'd look at him, see how great he was with the boys, and think how supportive he'd been of my career, and realize I needed to find a better balance between my job and my family. Maybe when this was over. Maybe when normalcy was restored.

He handed me the paper and gestured to a headline under the fold on the bottom half. "You need to read this."

I looked at him and smiled hesitantly. Then my eyes drifted to the story, and the headline: "VA official in Arizona demoted after her testimony."

I could not believe it. My spirit soared as I kept reading.

"A longtime spokeswoman for the U.S. Department of Veterans Affairs in Arizona has been removed from her post," Dennis wrote, "allegedly because she breached security by asking her husband to upload photographs of the Phoenix Veterans Day Parade onto a secure government website.

"Paula Pedene, a 23-year employee with the VA Health Care System, is fighting her reassignment to the hospital library, claiming she is a victim of reprisal by current administrators for testimony she gave against former administrators who left their jobs amid federal inquiries, according to records obtained by The *Arizona Republic.*

"Pedene's legal advisers and VA records indicate the dispute stems from a larger controversy involving years of mismanagement, squandered funds, discrimination, sexual harassment, and retaliation at the Phoenix VA.

"Pedene, the Veterans Day Parade coordinator since 1997, was notified of her transfer in a Dec. 10 letter from Associate Director Lance Robinson. He wrote that she was the subject of a 'very serious' allegation, and he issued a gag order prohibiting public disclosures.

"Pedene declined to comment. But her defenders said the investigation constitutes thinly disguised retribution for sworn statements Pedene made about misconduct by previous administrators in Phoenix who quit the agency amid federal investigations…

"Joseph Abodeely, an attorney for Pedene, sent another letter to Robinson on Feb. 11 demanding that she be returned to her job. Abodeely noted that Pedene's husband is an authorized VA volunteer who was asked by his wife to post photographs on the agency website because of his wife's disability. Pedene is legally blind. Abodeely criticized agency administrators for treating that event as a 'heinous breach of security.'

"You have unjustly embarrassed, humiliated and defamed Paula Pedene long enough," he added.

"Former Maricopa County Attorney Rick Romley, who chairs the Parade-sponsoring Honoring Arizona's Veterans of Phoenix, said he authorized Pedene to hire her husband as a photographer (*for the Parade*) and cannot understand VA administrators' response to a seemingly minor transgression.

"'Quite frankly, this is peanuts in the security world,' said Romley, who in 2006 served as special security adviser to the Secretary of Veterans Affairs in Washington. 'At the most, she should be orally counseled. She is so committed to veterans, it's just unbelievable. ...Nobody questions her sincerity in wanting to do things right.'"

Dennis went on to recount the issues under Reyes and Beam and noted that I had been interviewed by a federal investigative board that was looking into the charges of misspending, sexual harassment, and a hostile workplace under their leadership. "She stood up and told the truth," Dennis quoted Roger. "It cost (administrators) their jobs, and they threatened to destroy adversaries and families."

You can't begin to know how I felt. This albatross had been removed from around my neck. For the first time since the ordeal began, employees, veterans, patients, and members of the community got the broader picture of what had happened to me and why.

I looked at Bill. He was beaming. There was joy in that smile, joy and love. We hugged each other tightly. Then, Bill being Bill, he ushered me out the door to catch my van.

Honestly, it had never dawned on me that my testimony about Reyes would come back to haunt me. I did what I thought was right. Dr. Sam Foote, the Thunderbird VA Health Care Clinic director who had originally called me to ask for help in exposing Reyes, and I had worked quietly, behind the scenes, to reveal the issues. Most of the staff had no idea we were collaborating, only that new leadership had arrived, and the hospital's ship was going to be righted.

When I got into the library, the atmosphere had changed. The skeptical looks and questioning eyes had vanished, replaced by high fives, thumbs up, grateful handshakes, and – from a surgery technician – a heartfelt "You rock." A lot of staff members came into the library and asked me to personally make them a copy of the article. I was so thankful that the pieces of the puzzle were starting to come together, and the picture that resulted bore little resemblance to the portrait of me that Lance had been painting. After months of enforced silence, I got my voice back.

That night, when I got home, the weight of it all hit it me. All I could do was cry. But this time, it was with both gratitude and sorrow.

My media victory would be short-lived, however. I knew deep down that the 6th floor leadership was not going to take this lightly. And Sharon, who had played an under-the-radar role in trying to sabotage the Parade, was about to come out of the shadows and throw a very public punch.

17

As the Hospital Crumbles, A Puzzle Surfaces

The *Republic* article changed everything. For the first time, people in my orbit – some of whom had stuck with me, others not so much – finally had some idea of what was happening. In an unintended way, the story also had the effect of lifting Lance's gag order. Since a few of the details were now public, I was free to talk about some things – though not everything. My legal team was advising caution, as they believed Sharon and Lance were still hell-bent on firing me. Still, I tried to keep a low profile and let Dennis Wagner's reporting speak for itself. On the other hand, my colleagues didn't feel constrained.

People inside and outside the hospital came forward offering to help. We suggested that they write Secretary Shinseki and the Arizona congressional delegation, and many did. Some went to the online version of the *Arizona Republic* story and posted their comments, calling what was being done to me a "travesty." There were even a few cases where they actually began questioning the leadership of the hospital in general, if not Lance and Sharon directly. With the climate of fear being what it was at the Phoenix

VA, much of the support was quiet and behind the scenes, as co-workers didn't dare speak to me or about me any place where word could get back to the sixth floor. But privately, in the deserted hallways and stairwells, I received assurances, with many saying they were praying for me. That meant a lot and would be a needed source of strength in the trying days to come.

The article also buoyed the spirits of my teammates in the vanpool. We had started our own personal ride-sharing service a year before, mostly as a convenience. But I don't think any of us knew that it would become a kind of group therapy, where we could talk freely, share information, give each other inspiration or advice, or just have the occasional laugh. It included people from across the hospital spectrum: a nurse practitioner, a pharmacist, a psychologist, a quality manager, an engineer, a health administration clerk, and a former public affairs officer (that would be me). Before the newspaper story hit, I couldn't tell anyone what was happening; they just knew I was out of my job. Combined with the rumor mill and water cooler conversations, I think that may have at least raised some doubts in their minds. But afterward, it was a new normal.

That didn't mean everything was sunshine and roses, however.

We felt the hospital was lurching into a crisis. Concerns were growing among staff that patient care was being compromised, and good health care professionals were leaving in droves. I knew about it first-hand because one of my jobs as a "temporary" library clerk was to make sure that employees returned books and medical journals they had checked out to the library before they departed the Phoenix VA. When they did transfer or leave, the library staff initialed a sheet that cleared them from their "indebtedness." I was doing a lot of initialing. In December 2013 alone, we lost 100 nurses. It was one of the most heartbreaking things I'd ever experienced during all of my years with the VA.

As you can imagine, this was quite the topic in our vanpool. It was no secret that conditions were worsening, and that Lance and Sharon bore much of the responsibility. But what was a secret, at least to us at the time, was that Sharon stood to get a $10,000 bonus if the objectives of her "Wildly Important Goal" program were achieved. WIG, as it was called, was developed by Franklin Covey. It consisted of four disciplines: focus on the wildly important goal; act on the lead measures, which according to the company are what you do to move you toward your wildly important goal; keep a "compelling scoreboard" that lets people know if they are winning or losing; and keep a "cadence of accountability," meetings that focus on the goals and the commitment to meeting them.

In other words, if Sharon set goals and then showed she was meeting them, she'd get her bonus.

But as I said, we didn't know any of this in the spring of 2013. We did, however, know that one of Sharon's "Wildly Important Goals" was to reduce the wait time between when a veteran called in for an appointment, and when a specialist could see him or her. That wasn't really surprising. VA wait times had been a concern for years, and the system across the country was looking for ways to shrink the gap between initial contact and arrival in the doctor's office.

The WIG program and wait time issues would pop up periodically in our vanpool. At some point, we learned that our Health Administrative Service clerk who rode with us, Pauline DeWenter, had been directed to start keeping a "paper-oriented wait list or 'logbook' for new appointments." Whether it was a veteran calling in for an appointment or a veteran enrolling for care in person, the information requests were being entered onto the computer and printed out, then deleted from the system. The stacks of patient appointment requests were being placed in drawers. One or two staff members were then reassigned to pick up the stacks from each of the clinics and call the veterans in an effort to catch up on the backlog of paper lists. I'm no mathematician, but you don't need to be a numbers wiz to see that when a wait list was growing by thousands, it was no match for a couple of clerks.

As I started to put the pieces of this together, two things kept nagging at me.

First, if Sharon was so obsessed with reducing wait lists, why were patient requests being hidden? As I have said, she ruled by fear; no one was going to do something like that on their own without an explicit directive from leadership. Was she trying to hide something?

And second, why was anyone even putting, let alone hiding, the information on paper? The VA had begun moving toward electronic lists a few years prior. Why hadn't the Phoenix VA?

It made no sense.

But it would.

Sadly, within a year, it would.

18
WEAPONIZING THE PARADE

In March 2013, after the story about me hit the *Republic*, Rick Romley received an email from Sharon saying she wanted some changes in the Veterans Day Parade. He thought it was a less-than-subtle effort to tarnish my image by, in some way, suggesting that what we'd done in the past hadn't worked.

Sure. This is what our "failure" looked like:

A Parade that started with ten entrants had grown to more than 110. We had over 1,000 volunteer participants. The hospital earned hundreds of positive media hits from the Parade and the run-up to it. Tens of thousands of people – some said as many as 45,000 – lined the Parade route to watch the event. There was an essay contest for high school students, and a breakfast honoring the winners, followed by visits to rooms in the hospital where the kids read their works to the patients. Veterans often listened to the students with tears in their eyes.

So, how did Sharon plan to improve on all that? By yanking the hospital's support for the Parade altogether, which meant the Phoenix VA would no longer provide staging areas or allow employees to work on the event, and it would not host the kinds of events and contests that highlighted our celebration of Arizona's veterans.

Rick had sensed something was going on after Sharon's first email. So, when I found out for certain that his and Katherine's concerns were real, I called Roger and asked what I could do. He told me to get back with Rick.

I had been fortunate in having Roger, Rick, and Joe Abodeely in my corner. They were tough, committed advocates who knew the difference between right and wrong, and understood we were a little David fighting a big, bureaucratic Goliath. They were not guys to be trifled with. But Sharon, apparently believing supreme power had been conferred upon her, didn't quite get that. To put it mildly, she'd engaged the wrong opponents.

I took Roger's advice and talked to Rick, who was furious. He called Dennis Wagner at the *Republic* to tell him what was going on with the Parade and how VA (or, more accurately, Sharon) was trying to sabotage it. On April 8, the story broke, headlined, "VA to pull sponsorship of Veterans Day Parade." In the piece, Rick said the move could be seen as retaliation against me for my testimony against Reyes and Beam. Stu Jones said the withdrawal had "nothing whatsoever" to do with that, instead claiming that liability concerns, finances, and manpower issues were behind the decision.

"Being a sponsor of an event of this magnitude has required the re-prioritization of hundreds of staff members away from our core mission of providing world class health care to our veterans, specifically in ensuring all veterans have access to care," he said in an email to Dennis. The concerns over liability stemmed from an incident in Midland, Texas, where a freight train hit a flatbed truck being used as a float, killing four veterans.

But – Sharon refused to be interviewed.

The hospital could not, or would not, provide details on the "hundreds" of Phoenix VA employees who had worked on the Parade nor the taxpayer expense for the volunteers, many of whom worked on their own time, not the VA's.

The core mission of the hospital seemed to be more about Sharon's ambition than providing world-class care for veterans, and morale was deteriorating by the day.

In the Texas tragedy, the railroad company – not the Department of Veterans Affairs – was sued, and the VA issued no guidance or directives in the wake of the accident.

I'm sorry, but the whole notion that this was about litigation concerns or finances or personnel was ridiculous. I can't say for certain if it was about me, but it sure felt like they were weaponizing the Parade. And if it walks like a duck and quacks like a duck and looks like a duck…Well, you get the point.

However, Sharon wouldn't let it go. She doubled down in an April 10 email to VA staff, saying, "…priorities in the organization (specifically access), and heightened awareness over liability concerns which VA Legal Counsel brought forward" drove the decision. At some point, though, she began to understand that she'd walked into a firestorm of her own making. But rather than simply issuing a public statement in the middle of her crisis (which would have been my advice), she thought it would be best to hit the airwaves and go on camera.

Terrible idea. One of the basic rules in media relations is to never make a bad story worse. Apparently, Stu Jones skipped that chapter in the PR 101 handbook, because Sharon's appearance was a disaster.

The report started with KPNX news anchor Mark Curtis saying that the Parade faced cancellation after the hospital's "sudden withdrawal" of its sponsorship. "This has left veterans outraged," he continued.

Then reporter Brahm Resnik came on. "Volunteer organizers say the VA is taking away the one person who makes the Parade run." Meaning me. Sharon must have loved that.

Cut to David Lucier, a Vietnam vet, who talked about how veterans were shunned when they returned from the war in the 1970s. "Now he sees a return to those days," Brahm stated.

"I think it's a pervasive attitude," David said, "a substantial shift in pervasive attitudes toward veterans."

Back to Brahm: "The loss of VA sponsorship meant the loss of the woman who's led the Parade's volunteer committee for fifteen years."

Then cut to Katherine Brooks: "It's a big loss, and we are not permitted to talk with Paula about anything…We have to bring Paula back into the loop. We can't take Paula out of the loop and have a successful Parade this year."

After Brahm noted that I was not allowed to speak to the media, he said he'd spoken with Sharon, and she "indicated" that I would not be back with the Parade, and that VA employees who had volunteered to help on hospital time would now have to do so on their own time.

She said her policy was to look closely at support for the Parade or other community events to ensure that "taxpayer money is spent wisely…And that is one of the reasons we want to make sure this is not a competing priority for any of the staff, and that they know health care access for veterans is No. 1."

The *Arizona Republic* also ran a story about VA pulling its sponsorship for the Parade. So, basically, Sharon said an event that veterans loved, that paid honor to and respected their military service, and that without question improved their psychological and emotional outlook was not a priority. She also insinuated that hospital staff, who mostly were volunteers, were wasting taxpayer dollars by participating. Unbelievable. And on top of that, supporters of the Parade were saying that it could not go forward without me, an argument that probably caused Sharon's head to explode.

While the fate of the Parade was up in the air, I went "underground" in an effort to save it. I say "underground" because leadership was watching me like a hawk. At this point, Joe, Rick, and Roger agreed I could volunteer to support the Parade on my own time, outside of VA working hours. So, Katherine became the front person, meeting with the Mayor to figure out some way to prevent Sharon from killing the event. While that discussion was going on, I was at another location with one of the mayor's aides (on my own leave time) because Katherine and I could not be seen together. Katherine was texting me questions that she couldn't answer, and I was answering them as quickly and stealthily as possible. It wouldn't be the first time I had to resort to spy tactics.

But it paid off.

The next day, the *Republic* reported that the City of Phoenix had stepped in to make sure the Parade went on after the hospital pulled out. Its investment would be about $85,000. Sharon had lost the media fight. Now she'd lost the Parade war.

And Sharon's comment about access for veterans being the No. 1 priority? That was about to enter the infamy hall of fame.

19
The Homefront

Even though we had begun to register some wins, like the *Republic* articles and saving the Parade, my depression wasn't lifting. It was hard enough coping with all the BS coming from Lance, Sharon, and their yes-people every day, but I also had to work overtime to keep myself from being buried in psychological darkness.

Most people who suffer from depression know they're down, but they don't always understand how the complete loss of hope can take over their thinking. That wasn't the case with me. I felt the misery and the gloom every day, and I felt the effects. What made it even harder was the fact that I'm not a negative person. I love my husband, my boys, my work, my friends – I love my life. So, in a way, I was fighting a two-pronged battle. One was against the hospital leadership. The other was against my own mind, as I struggled to not be consumed by pessimistic thoughts that would make the situation even worse.

It wasn't easy. I could feel the boys drifting further and further away. Steven would retreat to his room and get lost in his world of video games. While we didn't know it at the time, he was teetering on the edge of bipolar disorder while finishing his senior year in high school. Robert was attending Paradise Valley Community College. He was mad about what was happening to me and could not understand how, after all the time and energy and commitment I'd put into my VA career, they could just remove me on a whim. It felt like he was retreating, too, except it was into a shell of my making. They were both going through troubled times at an impressionable moment of their lives, and their mother was absent. That just killed me.

Bill, the kindest, most decent man I have ever known, was feeling the strain as well. He suffers from generalized anxiety disorder, where a person constantly and excessively worries about any number of things, like money, family, or work. I wasn't making his life any easier because those were exactly the kinds of things that kept us up at night. He was often angry while this mess was going on, so angry his blood pressure would go through the roof. I could see it in his red face. And why wouldn't he be? The weight of our life was on his shoulders. The house, the kids, paying the bills, managing the day-in day-out routines that keep a marriage and family on the right track. I was offering little in the way of emotional support, internalizing my pain and trying fruitlessly to get out from under the gray cloud that my medications were not lifting.

One night I walked into the kitchen. Bill was sitting at the table with stacks of envelopes and a checkbook. The financial pressures were intense. The VA had an army of lawyers, paid for by taxpayers, to fight me. Bill and I were paying for everything out of our own pockets, and it was starting to seriously add up. Our credit card debt was mounting, and we had been talking about taking out loans or a second mortgage on the house. I could see the concern – maybe even the desperation – on his face. He just looked at me, then at the piles of bills. "I'm not sure how we're going the be able to pay all these, and the lawyers," he said.

"I have an idea," I snapped. "GET MORE MONEY!!!" Then I took my wine and walked out. Not my finest hour.

I cried a lot during this period. I drank a lot. I was on the phone a lot, with Joe and Roger, or anyone who would listen. Talking about what was happening was therapeutic for me, but the people I told had differing reactions. Some were angry. Some were dismayed. Some were distant. It was as if my shrinking circle of friends and colleagues settled into three camps: Those who supported me; those who were afraid to talk to me; and those who decided to turn against me and take every opportunity to throw me under the bus. This last group was especially upsetting because I'd known some of those people for more than twenty years. I didn't like it, but I guess I understood. Loyalty only goes so far in the face of leadership's fear-based management style.

I remember one time being in the hospital's basement lobby area and seeing an old friend walking toward me. We went way back. I had helped her when she first started in the job, talked with her often, and worked with her supervisors to find ways to support her career. As she approached, I stood in front of her, jokingly blocking her path. I laughed and said, "Hello, there." She didn't say a word or even acknowledge my presence. She just veered around me and walked off. The same kind of thing happened with another longtime friend who worked with the VA in another state. Over the years, we'd spoken frequently on the phone and attended meetings and training sessions together. When he was in town, we'd go to dinner or a Diamondbacks game. But after all this craziness started happening at the Phoenix VA, he dropped out of my life, as did his office colleagues. Roger had told me on more than one occasion that this nightmare would reveal who my true friends were. He was right.

In the midst of all this, I began to suffer from a spiritual crisis.

I have possessed a strong faith in God most of my life. I grew up Roman Catholic, living by its teachings and bringing a number of people into our church. But as my ordeal continued, and especially as the toll on Robert, Steven, and Bill increased, I began to question my beliefs. It wasn't as though I felt God was abandoning me, but I just kept asking why: Why was this happening? Why was this taking so long? Why aren't my prayers being answered? We had a mountain of worries – family, career, health, job, finances, the case – and I was trying hard to leave them in God's hands. There were times when I could not help but think they were slipping through His fingers. It was painful.

I'm not proud of the way I dealt with all of this at the time. I had always felt like I was a strong person, someone who could face – and face down – adversity with courage and grace. But I wasn't showing much strength. Instead, I was feeling depressed, anxious, withdrawn, and abandoned, and was terrified of being forced into an early retirement with a delayed pension or otherwise losing my job (and my sanity). Even so, I somehow managed to maintain hope that there had to be a way out of this, and I would find it. I had to. Every time I felt like throwing in the towel and walking away, and there were a lot of them and would still be a lot more of them in the months to come, I could not bring myself to do it. While yes, in my darker moments I wondered if God would ever again open His arms to me, somewhere deep in my heart I just knew He had a plan and would reveal it. When that happened, the long journey back to my life would begin.

And it did, thanks to an angel named Amy Voelker.

20
THE ANONYMOUS LETTER

A my was a fun-loving, care-free spirit who was one of the happiest and most joyful souls I had ever encountered. I'd known her for some time, but we really bonded in the vanpool. Her heart was bigger than her smile, and that was really saying something. When Roger told me that the battle against Lance and Sharon would sort out who my friends were and were not, Amy landed squarely in the friend category.

She was a pharmacist at the hospital and had seen first-hand how morale and care were beginning to crumble. She had watched as patients who were admitted for either physical illnesses or mental health issues were arbitrarily assigned to providers who had no experience managing their conditions and were then discharged with a month of meds and instructions to call back for an appointment when they ran out. She was concerned that some of those patients would just go off their prescriptions when they realized how hard it was to make those appointments. She also knew that some patients were stockpiling their medications, and even selling them.

Amy wasn't happy about any of it. When she'd had enough, she decided to do something and asked me to help. It's funny. During the previous few months, with Lance's gag order firmly in place, I had not really stepped up to make my concerns about conditions at the hospital clear. What discussions I did have, especially after the newspaper articles were published, were basically confined to me and my experiences. On top of that, I was not "in the trenches" like Amy and the providers were, so I only knew what people were telling me or talking about without actually experiencing it. Helping Amy felt like a chance to really make a difference by doing something directly related to patient care rather than to my own personal battles.

Amy had seen a lot, and she had a lot to talk about. Her plan was to write a detailed and comprehensive letter describing how patient care was suffering. My job was to edit her first draft and assist with a rewrite, and then develop a list of people we wanted to mail it to. Of course, this raised all kinds of potential dangers. If Lance and Sharon got wind of who sent it, we'd both be fired. If any of the examples we used could in any way lead to the identification of patients, we'd be fired. If we named names among Phoenix VA staff who were also concerned, they'd be fired. Given Lance and Sharon's track record when it came to going all scorched earth on anyone who crossed them or threatened their ambitions, it seemed likely they'd stop at nothing when trying to find out who was behind the letter.

We knew that. But we also knew that if we got our concerns in front of the right people, and included enough specific information, we stood a chance of having someone from either inside or outside VA send a team to Phoenix and start the process of correcting the hospital's slide. So, we decided the letter would be anonymous and would focus on what Amy had witnessed; my problems would be an afterthought at best.

The letter was dated April 17, 2013 and was titled "Hurting Patient Care." It was, to say the very least, scathing. It detailed a laundry list of crises: problems with monthly drug prescriptions; increased pressure on the Phoenix VA's specialty clinics, forcing them to diagnose and treat conditions their providers were not trained or equipped to deal with; professionals having to diagnose and treat patients they had never seen, with limited information and inadequate time; patients experiencing adverse drug effects because they were not being monitored properly.

Amy also included forty-four specific cases showing just how toxic the hospital's workplace had become: a provider who had just given birth asking for an extension of her maternity leave and being told that she had to show up immediately or resign; a nurse practitioner dropped into a new environment who, when she asked for orientation, was told her resignation would be accepted; overworked nurses; staff members who died from drug overdoses; employee suicides.

"Chaos," Amy wrote, "was the word of the day." The staff, she said, was "war-weary."

In addition to providing details on how the hospital was starting to unravel, Amy disclosed problems with patient access. She discussed how Sharon had shut down the hospital's Saturday clinic – which was used to handle overload and quickly get critically ill patients to specialty providers – without providing any option for replacing it. "(P)atient access rapidly declined," she wrote. "There was a point when the first appointment available was nine months out, and now some appointments may take as long as a year." When staff tried to at least put a Band Aid on the wound by scheduling patients early in the morning or late in the day during the week, they were "prohibited because the director threatened that the use of overtime would negatively impact their performance evaluations."

Keep in mind, this came at a time when Sharon was touting progress in her Wildly Important Goal of increasing access. Except access was getting worse, not better, and we were pretty sure once that bubble was burst, and officials saw the contrast between what she was saying publicly and what she had to know was occurring behind the scenes, she'd be called to account for it.

After finalizing the letter and sending it to Roger for review – he assured us it was fine – we decided to send copies to the VA Office of the Medical Inspector in Washington, D.C.; the Office of Quality Monitoring of the Joint Commission in Chicago, which accredits U.S. health care facilities including VA nationwide; the VA Office of the Inspector General in Washington; and Secretary Shinseki. That's when things got a little dicey for me and, frankly, kind of comically cloak-and-daggerish.

I wrote earlier about how paranoia sometimes got its hooks in my head, so you can imagine everything that was swirling around up there as we went through all this letter writing. Working on the letter was one thing; that was just Amy and me, and I knew I could trust her. But sending it out to high-level VA officials – even as "anonymous" – was something else. Sure, we had done everything with an overabundance of caution, including writing it on our personal time, using only our personal computers and emails, and spending our own money on whatever supplies we needed. But I was fighting to get my job back. Even the smallest slip-up would come back to haunt me, and knowing that I was at the top of Lance's "Most Wanted List" had turned me into someone who spent a lot of the day looking over her shoulder.

So, I couldn't be too careful. That's where the cloak-and-dagger stuff came in.

Since I can't drive, Bill took me to Office Max to buy paper, envelopes, adhesive labels, stamps, and a water stick to seal the envelopes, so we didn't have to lick them. (Couldn't leave any

DNA traces, right?) We had some unused latex gloves in the house, and I put them on when I was creating the labels and prepping the letters for mailing. (No fingerprints.) I even set up a "top secret" room in the house where I could get everything together before sending out the packages.

Once we'd finished, I put the letters (still wearing gloves) into a bag that no one had touched, then put the bag in my briefcase. I suppose we could have mailed them from anywhere, but we felt that sending the letters from the hospital campus would provide some authenticity. That was a problem, though. I was convinced everyone was watching me, in the library and from the sixth floor. We needed someplace off the beaten path but still inside the hospital's zip code. Amy and I decided on the blue post office box right outside the Ambulatory Care Clinic front entrance. So, we asked the vanpool driver to take us there.

While Amy and another vanpooler we could trust held the mailbox door open, I looked around to make sure the coast was clear. Then I shook the letters – the four we'd decided on and a fifth to Dennis Wagner at the *Republic* – out of the bag and into the box, ensuring that not one of them was touched by anybody. We checked to make sure the letters were safely inside, glanced around again with our best we're-not-conspiring look, then scurried off to work as quickly and innocently as we could. I have to admit, Amy and I were both smirking when we walked into our offices that day.

For all of the risks and the James Bond shenanigans, I had no doubt we'd done what was necessary. It felt good, too, and gave me a sense of purpose, even progress, at a time when I was suffering from a lack of both. Even though Secretary Shinseki had not responded to any previous requests for an investigation of the practices in Phoenix, I thought our letter contained enough specifics to at least set off some alarm bells and get the ball rolling.

It did.

Except the ball didn't roll.

At first, it looked like our secret agent act paid off.

The following week, VISN18 – the Veterans Integrated Service Network, whose eight systems, including Phoenix, provides a range of care to veterans – sent a team to the hospital. One thing in our letter caught their eye: the existence of a paper list for appointment requests which, as I said, was not standard operating procedure at VA. But somehow, hospital leadership got wind of what we'd written and knew a VISN review team would be coming onsite to investigate, and the more ethically challenged members of the hospital staff leaped into action. A management team that had been so concerned with granting overtime suddenly authorized mandatory overtime so the names of those on the paper list could be entered into the electronic waiting list – something that should have been happening all along. The order of the day was that there were officially no paper lists, nor would there be if anyone asked. So, when the VISN team arrived, none of the paper lists were to be found. Rather than dig any deeper, the investigating team just said it would "monitor the patient waits and delays."

As events would prove, they didn't. And the edict to use only electronic lists would be quickly forgotten.

Strike one.

The week after the VISN team came and went, the Joint Commission – which, as I said, accredits hospitals – staged a "surprise inspection." Investigators interviewed our vanpool driver, Pauline DeWenter, who oversaw the lists in one clinic. She told them, quite clearly, about the paper lists and how management was using them to hide the patients' actual waits and delays in scheduling appointments. Unlike the VISN, which accepted what it was spoon-fed by the hospital, the commission wanted proof. Pauline said she had it.

She first went to the clinic where she worked and opened the drawer where the paper lists were kept. Mysteriously, they had vanished.

She apologized and took them to a second clinic. The lists had vanished from there as well.

At a third clinic, the clerk apparently hadn't gotten the word to get rid of the paper lists, so the Commission team found them. But after going all over the hospital for days, they didn't find much else. Even though some staff members affirmed the lists did exist in the various clinics, others outright lied and said they did not. In the absence of overwhelming evidence, it looked like the paper lists were the exception rather than the rule. The team didn't even conduct an exit interview before leaving, which experience told me was a sure sign something wasn't quite right.

So, again, no action. Strike two.

Next, there was this slightly bizarre "in-depth" employee assessment by a team from the VA National Center of Organizational Development, or NCOD, which evaluates things like workforce engagement and employee satisfaction. They were ostensibly there to look into staff morale and to talk to people about anything they were hearing or seeing. Sounds perfectly normal. So why "bizarre"?

Well, because I was "randomly" selected to be one of the employees interviewed. When I got the letter from Sharon informing me of this honor, I almost choked.

Think about it. I had blown the whistle on the previous administration. I had been the focus of newspaper articles that were less-than-friendly to the current administration. And I was accused of all kinds of misdeeds and was currently the subject of a 30-day investigation that had slogged on for months. Why on earth would Sharon have me talk about employee morale?

That's an easy one. It was a fishing expedition, a ploy to gather information from me about the case we were building against the hospital. The interview was designed to help them learn what I knew.

Roger, Joe, and I all agreed that was leadership's true intention. So, we decided that when I spoke to NCOD, I'd keep the inner workings of my case out of it and give up just enough information to let them know we were onto Sharon's wait list charade.

I sat down with the NCOD team leader, and boy, was it a game of cat and mouse. After about a minute, it became clear that she was about as interested in my observations about employee morale as I was in nominating Lance for the Nobel Peace Prize. Her interview went on for hours. She poked and prodded, and thanks to brilliant coaching from Roger, I was able to deflect every arrow. Maybe it was just my imagination, but it sure felt like I was getting the third degree and she was trying to cross me up, confuse me, or get me to stumble – anything to give leadership a window into what we were thinking.

No luck. I followed my instructions from Roger and Joe. Just the facts and the truth. The good news about telling the truth is that you never have to second-guess it – or yourself. You tell it over and over, and it never changes.

One thing bothered us all, though. Given how the interview had gone, and our shared belief that it was more about me than just employee morale, we had to wonder: Would any of what I said find an official audience? We couldn't be sure, but we didn't want to take any chances. Since the NCOD interview had been taped, we wrote a letter that restated everything I had said, just to get it on the record. It detailed the staff's lack of trust in the hospital leadership; poor performance and questionable unethical practices by the people in charge, notably Lance and Sharon; a "poisoned culture" and "brut management" style; efforts to remove staff members who did not toe Lance and Sharon's unethical line; and included a brief recounting of the retaliatory practices I continued to face. I closed it by saying that it would "take years to undo what these people have done, and are continuing to do, to drive the hospital into the ground." I doubt that Sharon would buy in to such a concept, since one of her former public affairs officers told me she's the "Instant Gratification Queen," and if you can't find a way to do it quickly as she asks, you'll be looking for a new job.

Unfortunately, but not surprisingly, the letter went nowhere.

I cannot say with any certainty that the "Hurting Patient Care" letter Amy and I wrote was behind the onsite visits that followed its mailing. Maybe the timing was coincidental. Nor do I have any proof that there was a conscious effort to bury what was going on at the hospital. However, the lack of action and follow-up by VA, the Joint Commission, and NCOD sure seemed odd. What was clear, though, and undeniable, was that no one seemed to be interested in a full investigation of the Phoenix VA and its leadership.

Sharon had dodged three investigative bullets. She had to be feeling like she was untouchable. And like most people who think they have the power to do anything they want, she decided it was time to vanquish her opponents once and for all.

Starting with me.

21

YOUR TRIAL IS COMING

May was anything but merry. If there was a light at the end of this tunnel, I was having an increasingly hard time seeing it. As I've said, I am a glass-half-full, the sun-will-come-out-tomorrow kind of person. But the glass was getting emptier, and I could not shake the sense that the sun was setting on me.

I sought refuge at my church, St. Patrick Catholic Community, with its beautiful music, caring people, and presence of the Holy Spirit. From the moment I walked through the door, I could feel the power of belief. I'd linger at the statue of Mary our Mother inside and tell her of my hopes and fears, and try to leave the issues that tormented me at her feet.

On several occasions, I went to the Well and Being Spa at the Fairmont Scottsdale Princess, whose beautiful healing environment wrapped me like a blanket. I'd get my hair done, take a yoga class, or go to the massaging waterfall, where I often cried when alone.

At night, while saying my prayers, I'd occasionally see a blue light that just appeared in the darkness. It calmed me, and gave me peace, as if maybe God was watching over me and reaching out, preparing me for the trials that would surely come.

Once, I had a premonition. I was in the library, helping Mark Simmons put books away. He gave me several to shelve at the far end of the room, close to a window. I put the first one up and turned to grab another. As I did, a sunbeam caught my face. In that instant, I had a vision of Lance and Sharon being escorted from the hospital campus. I could hardly believe what I saw and thought it would never happen. After all, they had been "winning" and I had been "losing," and there wasn't much indication that would change.

I told Mark, my supervisor, what I'd seen and how I felt. He looked at me oddly but intently. Then I excused myself and went out to call Bill and Roger and told them. Neither knew what to say. I don't know if they believed me or thought I'd finally cracked. But it didn't matter. I saw what I saw. It was a rare moment of hope in April of 2013.

By this time, my life was stagnating. I'd fallen into a pattern of drudgery that just sapped the energy, joy, and enthusiasm from my body. Everything that had been so much a part of my identity at VA had been taken away. The daily executive meetings. Handling media inquiries. Setting up tours of the hospital and visits by elected officials. Mentoring and advising colleagues. I was in exile. While my colleagues in the professional public relations community outside of the Phoenix VA were doing whatever they could to advocate for me – writing letters to the Arizona congressional delegation and Secretary Shinseki – nothing was breaking through. I wasn't really surprised. I was among the first on-the-record VA whistleblowers facing this degree of retaliation.

We were in uncharted territory, and no one in a position to do something was going to back my cause until they could see a clear path forward. So, all I could do was keep my chin up, my nose clean, and my head down, and just keep waiting – which has never been one of my strong suits.

I was not handling any of this very well, so I decided to use some of the nearly 1,000 hours of sick leave I'd accrued for mental health days. When I called in for the third day, Shelby Roy answered the phone. She said I'd already been out for two days, and as this would be the third, I would need medical documentation to justify my continued absence. No problem. I talked to my counselor, who said he'd prepare a letter detailing my levels of stress and duress and explain how both were contributing to my depression. He wrote it up and sent it to Shelby.

She dismissed it, saying I needed a note from a medical doctor not a licensed counselor.

Fine. I got one. She still wasn't satisfied.

She went on to cite the fact that I'd taken seven percent of my available leave during the previous five months, and if that "meager" usage continued, I'd be put on leave certification. She was basically saying I could not be trusted to manage my time or leave, that I'd need a doctor's note for every day of sick leave I took, and that she would be monitoring both my sick and annual leave.

This made absolutely no sense. She was forcing me to jump through hoops when asking for leave, then punishing me for not taking enough leave. It was crazy. I called Roger, and he said that from a human resources perspective, she couldn't do that. But he also said this wasn't about what was right or wrong in the HR context. This was harassment. Shelby's responsibility, explicit or otherwise and no doubt assigned to her by Lance, was to make me miserable and to do what she could to force me to quit. This was just another petty tactic in leadership's war of attrition.

The beat goes on. Like President Reagan said, "There you go again."

Late in May, I attended a retirement reception for Susan Colvin, a supportive longtime colleague who was the Assistant Chief of Health Administration Service. After it was over, I went back with her to her office. We walked in. She closed the door.

"You know that Lance is looking for ways to get you out." I nodded. "Well, I've heard he asked Janet Adams to conduct a random audit of your spending from your public affairs control point. She's been told to find something he can use against you, and to do it quickly."

I thanked her for the warning and left. I'd find out later about the Lance-Janet plot, but this was the first time I'd heard about it. I was a little anxious, but I also knew they weren't going to find anything because any spending was done according to the rules and with the approval of my bosses.

You'd think after all these months, and everything Lance had done, that I'd be a little less naïve in thinking the system was actually fair and worked the way it was supposed to. This wasn't how the government, *my* government, was supposed to operate.

Whatever illusions I may have had were soon shattered.

I was riding in the car with a friend who told me leadership was moving ahead with an Administrative Investigative Board, or an AIB, with the intent of disciplinary action against me. It would focus on spending for the Parade, for employee and patient recognition items, for expenses related to a TV show I produced, and a host of other alleged offenses. Lance and Sharon wanted me out. Getting the AIB finding they needed would give them an official justification for doing it.

"Everything I did with funding was done by the book," I told her.

"Doesn't matter. They don't care." She hesitated for a second. "And Paula, there's one more thing."

"Okay."

"They're going after the security breach, too."

"My logging Bill on? They know there's nothing to that!"

She clammed up. "Like I said, they don't care."

She hung up. I took a moment to compose myself and try to absorb what she had said and what it meant. Then I got Joe and Roger on the phone.

"Get ready," they both said. "Your trial is coming."

22
THE KANGAROO COURT IS NOW IN SESSION

"Administrative investigations" are defined as the process designed to "determine facts and documenting evidence about matters of significant interest to the VA." They're governed by two documents. The first, Directive 0700, sets out the policy framework for conducting them. The second, Handbook 0700, describes the procedures to be followed when undertaking the investigation.

Directive 0700 states the following:

"Investigations that fail to adequately address critical issues, or that reach findings, conclusions, or recommendations that are not supported by the evidence, are an ineffective use of resources and can adversely affect the operations of VA's facilities, the morale of its employees, and its image before Congress and the public."

According to Handbook 0700:

"Convening authorities shall select members (of the Administrative Investigative Board) who are impartial and objective with respect to the subject matter;

111

"Board members shall maintain 'objectivity, impartiality, and professionalism'; '(o)bjectively, carefully, and skillfully analyze evidence'; and be 'objective and impartial' and not have a 'personal interest or other bias with the respect to the investigation';

"The board 'should attempt to review all available documents, records, and other information that are material to the issues of the investigation'; and

"The decision whether to convene an investigation should not be made by an official whose own actions (or failure to act) are likely to be the subject of the investigation, or who appears to have a personal bias in the matter to be investigated."

So basically, these two documents – even though they might sound like a bunch of self-preservation (and self-serving) bureaucracy-speak – make a promise that when an employee is hauled in front of what amounts to an internal VA court, he or she will get a fair hearing. Keep that in mind when you see what happened next.

I was sitting at my desk on June 5 when two people walked into the library and asked me to step outside the door. One was Robert Scott, Sharon's administrative assistant. The other was Julie Cain, the administrative assistant to Dr. Darren Deering, the medical center chief of staff. They presented me with the notice that I was going to be the subject of an Administrative Investigation Board "for the purpose of conducting a thorough investigation into the facts and circumstances regarding inappropriate employee behavior." I was to show up at Room 239, Building 26, on June 10. Why it took two people to serve me, let alone two people who seemed to be puppets of top hospital leadership, was anybody's guess. Mine was that it was an attempted show of brute intimidation.

Under normal circumstances, you'd think I would be rattled. That would come later. But in that moment, all I felt was anger. The notice came more than six months into my "30-day investigation," and during that time, the rumor mill – already grinding – had picked up even more speed, with whispers (and non-whispers) about privacy breaches, illegal use of government funds, and accepting gifts. Lance and Sharon seemed to think the longer they could string these accusations out, the more the pressure would mount on me, and the more likely I'd be to cave in.

I also received a "charge letter" that stated the allegations the AIB would examine. When I showed it to Joe and Roger, they seemed a little optimistic. The "inappropriate" behavior was limited to only two things: my logging Bill onto the computer, which as far as I was concerned was absolutely by the books; and the purchase of a $50 AM/FM radio for my office, an expenditure that had been approved and was perfectly appropriate for the public affairs function. I, on the other hand, didn't share their halfway rosy outlook. I remembered the heads up I'd gotten from Susan and my other "source" about the volume of issues they were looking into and told my two reps we needed to be ready for more. As I was nervous, I asked Joe to put me through a mock question and answer session a day before the board convened. That exercise made me feel a bit better. I mean, the truth was on my side. All I had to do was tell it, right?

Not exactly.

Sharon had made the decision to convene the board, then hand-selected the chairman and members. (So much for someone not making the call who "appears to have a personal bias in the matter to be investigated.") It became obvious, and pretty quickly, that her picks were not what you'd describe as "sympathetic" to my case. Runa Herra*, the Chair, was blunt in her opening remarks: "This board has been appointed by the Director to conduct a thorough investigation into the facts and circumstances regarding allegations that you engaged in inappropriate behavior in relationship to information security and misappropriations violations."

There it was: Bill and the radio.

Demi Small, a member of the board, got things rolling. "The alleged security violation was: You allowed Mr. Pedene to log on to your computer and allowed Mr. Pedene to use the computer with your logon name. Thus, this log on of a volunteer to conduct work on your behalf on an official VA computer is one of the violations."

I was prepared for that and patiently explained that because of my previous whistle-blowing activities, the administration had cut my staff and budget, so I had to use volunteers. I recounted how my former assistant, Anna Laurel, had checked with the Privacy Office and been told that volunteers could log on to a VA computer if they were supervised. I reminded them I am legally blind, and that Bill was a registered VA volunteer, and that I'd asked him to do something that was challenging for me to do – put pictures into a PowerPoint – "so I considered it both a support and accessibility issue." I told them the presentation in question was a public document, that Bill was under my supervision, and that he had no access to any other files or folders.

So, my reasoning was grounded in facts, and given what the Privacy Office had told Anna, there was a foundation for allowing Bill to use the computer.

Facts and foundation weren't good enough for Runa Herra, though. "Did you ever have a conversation with the Privacy Officer yourself to validate if that was indeed an acceptable practice?"

This was starting to feel like a setup. "I did not."

"Okay, thank you."

A few moments later, another board member, Dan Adam, came at me from another direction. "Do you happen to remember if you were – at the time that this was happening – if you, yourself, were current on your privacy awareness and security training?"

That flustered me. "Probably, but I don't remember." This came out of nowhere. My training had never been an issue because I was simply following a precedent my ex-assistant had cleared with the Privacy Office. Maybe my paranoia was coming back, but it sure seemed like someone had fed him that question.

He didn't follow up, instead pivoting to the second issue in the charge letter I'd received. "That dealt with the fact that you have participated in or permitted the use of appropriate funds to be used in a manner and purpose that was not permissible under Appropriations Law or VA financial policy –"

I interrupted him immediately. I held up the charge letter I'd received. "It says that I am being called to appear before the board for inappropriate employee behavior and the purchase of a radio, but no other purchases are mentioned. Those are the only charges I'm aware of."

"Wow," he said. "Okay." Like this was all news to him.

"So, I just want to state for the record that I have been provided one piece of paper and two charges."

But here they were, trying to expand the accusations to include things that were not in the scope of their charge letter.

Unless, of course, they'd been coached.

They fumbled around on that one for a minute or two, then moved on to the $50 radio.

"You purchased a Memorex radio on July 17, 2012, for your office?" Demi Small asked.

I told her I had.

"These things appear to not be proper," Dan Adam said.

I explained to him that as a public affairs officer, I had a responsibility to monitor the news, and that my requests for cable TV in my office had never been acted upon. "The radio was the only option I was provided for news monitoring. As there had been several protests at the park next door recently, which was impacting patients and staff access to VA, along with regular news that could touch upon veterans issues, the purchase was authorized as part of my job function. So, yes, I purchased the $50 radio for the office. It's government property."

With that, they concluded the interview. I'd been in front of the board for less than an hour. I'd admitted what they already knew, explained my reasons, and told the truth. Joe was satisfied. He didn't think there was any way they'd push back harder.

Roger and I weren't quite so confident. There was something about the nature of the questions – the board members seeming to know more than they were alluding to and seeking to trap me into discussing issues not included in the original charge letter – that didn't feel right. Call me paranoid (again), suspicious, whatever. But something was off.

Two days later, they yanked me back before the board. I was about to learn, and quickly, that what Freud once said was true:

The paranoid is never entirely mistaken.

23
THE FIX IS IN

On day two of my testimony before the AIB, it was clear: The fix was already in motion.

When I walked back into the hearing room, there was a huge stack of binders and paperwork on the conference room table. Between my initial appearance and the second, three days later, VA had interviewed fifteen witnesses (the usual suspects). What had started as an investigation of two issues – logging Bill onto the VA computer and my approved purchase of a $50 radio – had swelled into a boatload of charges.

Dan Adam handed me what he called "a generic listing of some financial transactions."

Joe jumped in, saying, "nobody's ever had the courtesy to provide us with this kind of notice to let us know" about multiple questions over the transactions.

Runa Herra: "That's why I'm letting you and your client review this now." Oh, so it's okay to withhold critical information and then give it up when it's not in my best interests?

This was clearly an ambush.

They questioned expenditures for the Parade going back over a decade. All of them had been approved by prior purchasing agents and fiscal officers. "Everything that is on that list was for VA recognition, VA outreach, VA involvement." I added, "We had six or seven fiscal officers during this timeframe. All of them concurred with those expenses." Then I noted it was interesting that the only fiscal officer who did not agree was the current one, Janet Adams, who, not incidentally, was serving under Lance and Sharon.

Ms. Herra, who clearly was out for blood, tried to set a trap. "So, do you believe after you've reviewed this list that these are appropriate expenditures, and you verified that you are the one that authorized these?" She was laying the ground to pin the decision on me.

Joe shut that down. "She stated that it was approved by other people."

But no matter how many times I reminded them that everything was on the up-and-up – even citing regulations to support my case – they didn't seem to care. They were on a mission of mercilessness. They demanded to know the names of the fiscal officer I'd talked to. They called me on that purchase of the yellow paper. I explained that the VA Veterans Day Parade was held on a day when businesses were operating, and that the VA was required to let citizens along the route know the streets would be closed to normal traffic so they could plan to use alternative routes. We used the yellow paper for the notifications. They asked me about the graphic design of the employee newsletter, which I had to do because Medical Media – which had the scope of practice to do so – told me they were too short-staffed and too busy to handle it. So, I found the way by hiring a minority-owned small business, which supported our purchasing standards.

I had the answers and told the truth. It didn't feel like I'd given them any ammunition. I mean, how many times, and in how many ways, can you say, "Everything was approved by my supervisors according to proper procedures"?

So, they went back to their happy place: My use of volunteers.

"It is customary to have volunteers here at the hospital," Ms. Herra said. "Did you have any volunteers working for you?"

I replied that I did, then went through the details of why I needed them: I used to have a staff of four and a $250,000 budget, but they were both slashed by Geoff Reyes, who said that if I wanted help, I'd have to get it for free. I explained to the board how, after Reyes "retired," the interim director asked me to prepare a memo seeking to restore the public affairs function that had been gutted. I told the board that this process of requests for restoration, including budget and staff, was happening every month from May until December 2011. My requests were never granted, despite the director's promise to do so.

Ms. Herra didn't care about the "why." She politely thanked me and said, "But, I believe I asked you what kind of duties they performed for you, the volunteers."

I wasn't giving her the information she asked for. But then again, this wasn't about what it was supposed to be. I pointed out once more that context was important, and that after his appointment as associate director, Lance had told me to stop asking for staff and budget and ordered me to quit talking about problems with the previous administration. "That's when I began looking for volunteers." Which, of course, brought the Board back to my husband Bill.

"Did you at any time log on a volunteer under your access?" Ms. Herra asked, knowing full well what the answer was.

"My husband. Yes."

"Was your husband a volunteer?"

"Yes."

"Can you tell me why you logged your husband on under your access?" I reminded her we'd gone over all that in the previous interrogation. "Can you refresh my memory?" I did.

Then the ground shifted beneath my feet.

She asked me if I was aware of something called the Phoenix VA Health Care System Policy Memorandum 13508 that she said stated that a spouse or relatives "can't work with other relatives in the VA if they are volunteers."

I hadn't. It was an obscure document that I'm guessing few people even knew existed.

But someone had fed it to the board. And the AIB was going to feast on it, and on me.

I pushed back as best I could, saying that Bill did not work for me, but for Medical Media, which had assigned him to Public Affairs.

Ms. Herra dismissed my argument. I told her about the PowerPoint, about Bill uploading the photos, the fact that there was no sensitive information involved, and that the presentation was a public document. "So, he had no access to any kind of patient information whatsoever?" I was thinking, didn't I just say that?

But I replied, "I don't go into patient records. That's not my role in public affairs." So, by extension, Bill had no access, either.

After some more back and forth on routine process matters, Ms. Herra returned to the subject of computer logons. I repeated that Anna, my former assistant, had confirmed with the Privacy Office that a volunteer could have access if they were properly supervised – as was the case with Bill – and that Anna had told me as much, and in fact had herself supervised numerous volunteers in the same manner.

Once again, Ms. Herra did not seem to care. "But you never validated that information?" She was clearly trying to set another trap, and I got the feeling that someone else was pulling her strings.

"If I made an error in judgment in trusting my staff, I made an error in judgment."

She pivoted again. "It's our understanding that your husband, Mr. Pedene, had administrator rights to Facebook."

Here it was. The posting of the patient photo after her makeover day.

"Yes," I said.

"And how did he get those administrator rights?"

"To upload photos?"

"Who granted him that access?"

"I did."

Then she showed me VA Form 10-3203, which authorizes consent for, among other things, use of pictures. I knew what it was. We had one for the patient whose picture we'd put on Facebook. It had nothing to do with Bill, but she seemed more interested in trying to throw a whole bunch of privacy charges against the wall – however unfounded and unconnected – and see what stuck.

I told her that a nurse on the ward had come to me saying she had a hospice patient we could help "feel special" if we gave her a makeover day. "She and her family were so pleased with what we did, they wanted to know if we could put the photos up on the Phoenix VA Facebook page," I continued. "I said the only way that we could do that is if we could get the patient to sign the consent. So, she (the nurse) went, she got the consent, then I uploaded the photos."

"Do you know that these photos were uploaded posthumously?"

Whoever was trying to set me up had their facts wrong. "No, they were not."

"They were not."

"They were uploaded the day that the patient and her family requested that they be put on Facebook."

Caught in a lie, she quickly moved on. "Is it normal procedure for us to accept the document with the X's on like this?"

I told her it was, and that in cases where the patient cannot sign, we have a witness, which we did, who would attest that the X represented a signature.

A few moments later, they changed direction again, coming after me over an intern that I'd had to let go because he wasn't up to the job. Ms. Herra asked if I had put him on a training path to become a public affairs specialist. I said I had. She didn't believe me. "We have received a statement that he was never afforded the opportunity to be trained."

That was utter nonsense, fake facts, someone's alternative reality.

I told her if I could get to my files, I could show that I authorized him to attend a web-management training program and approved educational programs for graphic design and PowerPoints and how to better manage his calendars. Of course, there was a problem with getting that information because Lance had taken away my computer access. How convenient.

The lies and crazy accusations continued.

Demi Small said I'd spent $440,000 on TV shows promoting the hospital. "No. No. No. No. I don't know where you got that figure." She didn't tell me.

Runa Herra then grilled me about a 40-foot-tall balloon we purchased for the Parade that depicted a doctor and was used to express our thanks to the 200-plus physicians at the hospital for the care they provided to veterans. "Community outreach for the VA," I said.

For some strange reason, she questioned my work with Honoring Arizona Veterans, which oversaw the Parade. I told them it was purely voluntary, something I did on my own time outside the office, as a disabled American veteran.

Her final question concerned the March 29 article in the *Republic*, which said I was demoted because of my testimony against the previous administration. "Can you tell me who told the press…that you had been removed from your post?" The inference was clear: I'd leaked it.

"I do not know who told them that," I replied.

She asked if Roger, my employee representative, had discussed my case with Dennis Wagner and given him the information. I said he did. "I thought you told me you had no idea," she shot back. I apologized for not being clear. I didn't say Roger was the leak, but good Lord, he was quoted in the article. Of course, he was a source. Were they just trying to catch me in a misstatement?

As the interview came to an end, Runa Herra asked, "Is there any other information you think we should know or people we should contact in order to secure all the facts of this situation?"

Oh, hell, yes.

I began by repeating what I'd said over and over again. Any expenditures were undertaken appropriately, with approval from my supervisors, according to VA policies and procedures and processed by contracting representatives and fiscal officers. I corrected testimony from others that I knew to be false. I reminded the Board that, regarding my use of volunteers, Lance had consistently told me that I would get no more staff or budget, and that he was always questioning my integrity and putting me down for no reason other than he could. Then I gave them the names of my witnesses who could confirm and elaborate upon what I'd said and provide the Board a side of the story it had not yet heard. There were eleven of them in all, including Anna; retired U.S. Navy Admiral James Symonds, who Anna had logged onto the computer a number of times; Madge Monzingo, Lance's former executive who saw him commit personal and frequent computer-related breaches of security procedures; and Susan Colvin, who could testify to Lance's order to Janet Adams to find something on me and quickly.

I was going to get my side of the story on the record, and believed that when that happened, truth would win out.

Naïve, Paula. Again.

The AIB didn't call any of my witnesses. Not one. It decided their testimony "would not be relevant." Really? The AIB heard charge after charge against me by more than a dozen of *their* witnesses. They did not stick to the initial outline of the investigation. They conducted a "routine" investigation that went back a dozen years. They accepted misrepresentations and lies as facts. They ignored important evidence that would have totally undermined the tales my antagonists were spinning. And they did it all even though Ms. Herra said at the outset of the investigation she wanted to give me the opportunity to present my position.

My basic rights, which Lance had already taken from me, continued to disappear before my eyes.

Left with no other recourse, Joe crafted a letter to the Board under my name that restated everything I had said, addressed our concerns issue by issue, detailed the background of my testimony against the previous leadership, and recounted Lance's abusive treatment of me and his efforts to weaponize the Parade. There was also some pretty pointed commentary. At one point, I said, "It appears that the AIB has been used as a 'tool' for retaliation because I am a 'whistleblower'." But there was another statement that I think really got to the heart of what was going on:

"I am concerned that this Board has received some improper guidance from the convening authority or Sharon's staff…and that the AIB is biased toward the convening authority and has been improperly prejudiced against me."

I wasn't being defensive. In fact, that is exactly what happened.

Sharon didn't seem to be content to put her sycophants in place. She apparently went to the Board, met with them, and told them the outcome she wanted. We didn't know that then, but we found out later. Sharon, and whoever she could convince to harm me, seemed to be hell bent on controlling this entire process and making sure its conclusions were her conclusions. There was no independence here. There was no objective search for evidence. There was no plan to uncover the truth. This was a sham and an outrage, executed by Sharon Helman, who seemed to think she was beyond reproach. VA Medical Center Directors have a vast amount of power and resources, and for some, they have egos as big as the Grand Canyon. Roger once said, "They think royalty has been bestowed upon them." To us, that was a good analogy for Sharon Helman in a nutshell.

So, all we could do was submit our letter for the record – appropriately titled "Statement of Facts" – and hope that reason and principle and decency would finally win out. We thought at some point, it just had to.

You know that saying – The definition of insanity is doing the same thing over and over and expecting a different result? That was us. Continuing to believe that this process was unbiased and that good would eventually win out.

About thirty days later, we'd realize we were still crazy after all these months.

24

WAIT. WATCH. AND DRUDGE ON.

In the absence of anything that looked even remotely like an unbiased AIB hearing – and because I was never given the right to confront my accusers – I resorted to the only option I felt I had: file a Freedom of Information Act request seeking all files, documents, and testimony related to the Board's investigation. Additionally, I asked for various other materials, including memos, letters, correspondences, emails, issue briefs, and other communications that might have some bearing on my case. I had no idea, even if my request were approved, whether it would affect what was going on. But if it were handled according to standard procedures, I could expect to get the documents within ten days. Then we'd see. However, I also knew VA could delay compliance. Given Lance's strategy to grind me down, that did not seem out of the question.

So, I waited, either for the FOIA documents to arrive or for the AIB ax to fall. It was horrible.

As I've said, I'm a doer, someone who is in perpetual motion and always trying to move forward and accomplish things. Give me a project, let me run with it, and you'll get something back with great results. Playing the waiting game is not something I'm very good at.

As the days and weeks passed, I was becoming more and more of a wreck. I'd call Roger and cry, complaining to him about the unfairness of it all, the delays, the trumped-up charges and fabricated "evidence" that AIB would no doubt use against me. I didn't understand why the anonymous letters hadn't gotten veterans off the paper list or why Sharon was still getting away with her lies about improving access to care for our nation's veterans. I worried about what are called "ghost panels," in which veterans were assigned primary care doctors who were not actively providing care, allowing VA to collect money for them under appropriations, despite the fact the patients weren't getting any treatment.

With every call, every concern, every sob, Roger's response was always the same: "Wait. Watch. And drudge on." That's what I did.

I set out to become the best library technician I could. Good luck with that. With each day that passed, I could see my job as public affairs officer disappearing from view. Some mornings, I could not drag myself out of bed and needed help just getting into the van. I called in sick more than I ever had, and I scheduled more vacation time and longer breaks – anything to avoid the crushing humiliation I felt at the hospital. Often at night, I'd console myself with phone calls, not only with Roger, but also with Joe and any of the few remaining friends who were still willing to lend me an ear. I'd open a bottle of wine, sit on the kitchen floor next to the phone charger, and weep with glass after glass of wine until the bottle was empty. Fortunately, it wasn't expensive wine. We'd buy it by the case.

Meanwhile, things at home were getting more and more difficult. Our expenses continued to pile up and now included my medical bills. As a veteran, I routinely chose VA as my health care provider. I'd done that for twenty years and thought everything they did for me was great. But now, I was at a place in my life (and in my head) where I didn't know who to trust. With my stress and depression issues, I wouldn't have put it past Lance and Sharon to find a way to use this against me and pull VA documents to verify it. Sometimes, in my darker moments, I'd wonder if someone at the hospital would actually access my medical records, get what information they could, and pass it along to Lance or Sharon, who would then dial up the pressure to push me out. Paranoia, again. I get that. But you can never be too careful.

I also knew I needed counseling and was fortunate to find it with a non-VA professional, Tony Rubin. He had several clients from the medical center. He couldn't believe what was going on there, and what the leadership was doing to employees. One day, he said he'd never in all his years of working with people, seen such decay in an organization. Tragic as the situation was in the hospital, this was uplifting. Someone on the outside recognized the catastrophes on the inside. He helped me think and gave me perspective – both of which had been in short supply and had felt like they were evaporating more and more every day – and he got me to realize there was a season for everything. This one, what I was enduring, was my season of growth.

The boys were paying a steep price with this experience as well. They really didn't have a mother. I'd become almost invisible, adrift in my own world, where the only thing that seemed to matter was my case and what I was going through. It's not like they didn't understand. I think they did. But they deserved a mother who was present and active and could manage her crises while also supporting her family. I deeply regret to say that at this point, I was not that woman.

Robert had moved to Flagstaff to attend Northern Arizona University. He later told us he felt I was going through enough, so without him at home, it was one less thing to worry about. But what he didn't know was how much I missed him.

His college track was something of a rollercoaster, mostly due to what I believed were negative influences of his girlfriend, who was a bit of a wild card, to put it mildly. He was having issues – learning about friendships and relationships, social skills, and the like – that any young man of his age had, and on those occasions when I'd show up in his life's picture, he'd often push me away. I can't blame him. Being a mom isn't a part-time job. You don't just beam in when it's convenient and beam out when it's not. I was not there to help him navigate the waters leading to adulthood. He was angry – at what was happening to me, and at me. I don't blame him for that, either.

Steven's bipolar disorder was worsening. The highs and lows were becoming more frequent and serious. Most of us have ups and downs, and we chalk it up to a bad day. Steven's condition amplified that ten-fold, and we were trying to find the right mix of prescription drugs, therapy, mood stabilizers, supplements, counselors, and psychiatrists. Meanwhile, we were dealing with hospitalizations, disruptive behavior, and the like. The pressure on Steven – and, honestly, on Bill, who as I said was shouldering most of the parenting by himself – was just brutal. No one his age should have to deal with what was eating away at us.

My family, so happy and strong, even with the challenges, was God's gift to me. But I could feel the joy slipping away, replaced by a heavy sadness. There was no getting over the sense that it was my fault.

As we reached the second part of July, it was kind of like taking two steps forward, then one step back.

On July 18, VA informed me that it had completed the search of my record request under the FOIA. The fee wasn't cheap, $571.07, but Roger told me to pay it. I did.

On July 20, Roger said he'd been talking with a fellow HR representative who was a specialist at creating whistleblower cases with the VA Office of Special Counsel. I had no real idea what a "whistleblower" was at the time, other than what I vaguely remember from training courses and the movies, but apparently, I was about to become one.

So those steps represented forward progress.

On July 22, I contacted Runa Herra, allegedly the out-for-blood AIB chair, to ask when the Board's findings would be given to me. She said the report and recommendations had been forwarded to the hospital leadership. So, Joe sent emails to Sharon, Lance, Maria Schmidt (Hayden HR director), and Mark Romaneski, VA's regional attorney. And Joe followed up with phone calls. All he got was Romaneski saying he'd try to get some answers to our written questions. We never did.

One step back.

Then came a giant step forward.

On July 30, the FOIA materials arrived. The hospital's campaign against me was about to blow up in its face.

25
CHRISTMAS IN JULY

If there was ever any doubt that Lance and Sharon seemed to be willing to do whatever it took to railroad me out of my job, the Freedom of Information Act documents confirmed it. They were a treasure trove of incriminating information against VA – like Christmas in July. It took us a while to go through everything. Roger said it was standard VA operating procedure to bury its critics in paperwork, and that's exactly what the agency was doing to me. Well, they were trying to bury the wrong person.

By the time we'd read all the documents, it was clear that leadership had knowingly engaged in a conspiracy to destroy me. The evidence was undeniable, including:

- There was the Dec. 6, 2012 email to Kim Tesh from the VA Network and Security Operations Center stating that logging Bill on to the computer "does not meet the criteria for a data breach" and that incident should be considered closed.

- We got confirmation that Lance had gone to the fiscal office and told Janet Adams to "find something on Paula, and quickly." She did, informing him in a Dec. 11, 2012 email that a random fiscal audit revealed "inappropriate purchases" for the Parade and other minor items. Nowhere did she say that these purchases had been vetted and approved according to VA policies and procedures.

- On Dec. 15, Lance told Janet she needed to finish her review quickly, as an AIB hearing was planned for the beginning of the year. He also raised the possibility of going back many years – it turned out to be twelve – to look for anything they could use against me. So much for a "random" audit.

- In an exchange with Lance on Dec. 18-19, Kim Tesh said she had learned about a patient's photo being posted on Facebook, calling it a new and additional privacy breach. She proposed amending the original complaint that the National Security Operations Center had denied, stating there was no consent form on file. There was, of course, but looking for it and finding it weren't convenient to their narrative.

- On Jan. 31, 2013, NSOC rejected Kim's appeal and closed the complaint – again – determining "no privacy breach occurred."

We had them cold. They had lied. They had deceived. They had covered up. It was right there in black and white and could not be denied. As far as I was concerned, it was game over.

But what I didn't know, what none of us knew at the time, was that the game had already been fixed.

After getting the FOIA materials, Roger and I agreed there was little likelihood I'd face criminal charges, as we had initially feared. Given that Joe Abodeely was a criminal lawyer, and he had done an excellent job getting us through the "criminal investigation" stage of my case, Roger felt it was important now to turn to someone who had experience with the VA Office of

Special Counsel, an independent (theoretically) investigative and prosecutorial entity that (theoretically) protects federal government employees from "prohibited personnel practices," such as whistleblower retaliation.

That someone was Stephanie Renslow.

She had years of experience in human resource and had spent a decade working on VA matters. So, Roger arranged an introductory phone call. I went for a walk around the neighborhood, cell in hand and wearing headsets, as we spoke. Stephanie's voice was strong but vibrant, and it didn't take long to see that she was a quick study who understood at the deepest level what was going on. I poured my heart out to her, explaining how I was being affected by what was happening, and telling her where we were now, where we needed to go, and what I needed from her. We connected emotionally. She joined the team and would become instrumental in our strategy for moving forward.

Unfortunately, though, our agreement to work together an on OSC whistleblower case meant I had to end the relationship with Joe. It wasn't easy. He had been a huge help, especially in his dealings with and comments to Dennis Wagner at the *Republic*. But he understood that he'd done his job and that we were about to engage VA on a different battlefield where alleged criminal behavior was no longer an issue. It saddened us both. We parted ways amicably.

It didn't take long for Stephanie to show the stuff she was made of. She came out blazing. On Aug. 9, after we'd spent a few weeks researching dozens of cases that had been fought and won for whistleblowers, we then filed ours. As I said, I had only the barest idea of what a whistleblower was. With this filing, I had officially become one.

She set the stage quickly, stating, "it is a prohibited personnel practice to take or fail to take, or threaten to take or fail to take, a personnel action because of a protected disclosure of certain types of information by a federal employee." From there, she cited elements that had to be present to show that the law had been violated, detailed disclosures that were protected under federal statutes, and laid out the personnel actions that violated the prohibition against whistleblower retaliation.

Then she provided a long list of facts that we felt proved Lance, Sharon, and their allies had all taken actions that, by any objective criteria, could collectively be seen as a reprisal due do my disclosures. She detailed at length how my case had unfolded: The charges against Reyes and Beam; the slashing of my budget; Lance's mean-spirited indignities and humiliations; weaponizing the Parade; the by-now-discredited computer logon issue; how NSOC had not once, but twice, denied the privacy violation claims against me, that the leadership knew about these details, and that I was never informed of their resolution; The AIB and how we were stonewalled looking for its findings.

Her summary bordered on white-hot:

"The environment in which Ms. Pedene is working is unacceptable on many fronts. It is not productive, unnecessarily stressful, at times threatening, intimidating, anxiety-producing, and harassing. For the last eight months, she has been subjected to a management team that has no boundaries and shows complete disregard for Ms. Pedene as a teammate. They continue to create a hostile work environment which, at a minimum, is disrespectful and at the outside illegal, injurious mentally, physically, and emotionally.

"Ms. Pedene has tolerated this behavior in an attempt to take the 'high road' and allow the process to 'right' the situation she has been put in by VAHCS Phoenix management. However, when it has now affected her health, potentially her livelihood, and her home life, Ms. Pedene is forced to act and demand a change. To allow this situation to continue for this disabled veteran and 23-year successful employee of the Veterans Affairs is shameful."

Yep, that pretty much summed it up.

Stephanie and I both felt we had made a strong argument for whistleblower retaliation. But I have to tell you, filing the case lifted me out of my depression. I felt my spirit, faith, energy, and hope returning – and discovered a well of anger, too. It was good to fight back, and to fight back aggressively. I'd need it, too, because back in the shadows where they operated, Lance and Sharon weren't even close to backing down.

26

MORE LIES. A SUSPICIOUS FIRING.
ANOTHER LETTER.

Filing the whistleblower case didn't just give me a kind of mental and emotional recharge. It also increased my frustration and level of alarm over the long waits we were witnessing as the patients tried to access their care, and even the deaths and suicides that resulted when veterans could not get the treatment they needed when they needed it. The sad thing was, pretty much everyone on the front lines was aware of the situation. They confronted it every day. The sadder thing was that Sharon Helman not only refused to acknowledge that the hospital was in a crisis, she flat-out lied about it.

At a Service Chief's Meeting on July 1, 2013, Sharon's Chief of Staff, Dr. Darren Deering, reported that access to mental health services was at 78 percent, which meant it was three points above the 75 percent target. From what I saw and heard this was just not true. Patients were being scheduled for March 2014 – eight months down the road – and the number of outpatient mental health providers had dwindled to thirteen. Fewer providers delivering more and faster service? No way.

According to the meeting minutes, Deering also reported that specialty care access was at 46.3 percent compared with a goal of 40 percent. We had contrary evidence that showed this was false, too. Patients on the wait list weren't even being scheduled for specialty care. It's hard to get care if you're not being scheduled.

It was the same story with his "facts" about primary care access. Deering said it was at 36.75 percent, just below the target of 40 percent and improving. I knew this was false because by July 26, there were 1,500 patients on the electronic waiting list who couldn't get in to see a doctor.

He concluded by saying, "By continuing on this track, the facility will likely meet our goal."

But it appeared as if Sharon wasn't only relying on surrogates to execute her campaign of what we were calling deception. In a July 3 email – and its jaw-dropping aftermath – it felt as if she was trying to cement her standing as someone who believed she had permission from celestial powers above to do whatever the hell she wanted.

She sent the email out to what she called the hospital "family", providing an update on the progress of her "Wildly Important Goal" access program. To call it misleading would be an understatement. She touted the same false numbers Deering had discussed July 1, saying there had been "extraordinary progress" in reducing wait times. She went on to reset the goal (buying time, really) for providers to see new primary care patients, setting a target of fourteen days from the time the appointment was created. By Sept. 30, she added, "more than 40% of our new patients in Primary Care will be seen within fourteen days of the date that their appointment is created."

"We can do this!!" she exulted. Sure. Like I said, it appears as if you can do anything if you are manipulating the data.

Here's how she closed:

"As we celebrate this holiday weekend, let's take a moment to reflect on those who have served and show them our gratitude. I truly appreciate your commitment to this mission and to our goal of providing timely access to healthcare for the veterans we serve."

Damian Reese, a social work analyst at the hospital, was having none of this. He pushed back hard. In a July 3 email to Sharon's executive secretary, he wrote:

"I think it's unfair to call any of this a success when Veterans are waiting six weeks on an electronic waiting list <u>before</u> they're called to schedule their first PCP (primary care physician) appointment. Sure, when their appointment is <u>created</u>, it's (sic) can be fourteen days out, but we're making them wait 6-20 weeks to create that appointment. <u>That is unethical and a disservice to our veterans</u>." (Emphasis in original.)

In response, he got a note back from Mary Treet*, the Associate Director of Patient Care Services, that was full of warm-and-fuzzy self-praise: "(W)e know patients are waiting, and we have plans to get them all seen as soon as possible"…"We have a lot of successes"…"Staff efforts are resulting in appointments available within two weeks for patients; some providers have appointments within a week, and some providers have same day access." An hour after sending it, Mary received an email from Sharon:

"I think this should also go as an admin ethics consult."

Okay, this is when things got interesting. Or maybe just more disgusting. Or maybe more evidence that Sharon thought she could simply roll anybody.

K.J. Sloan, who was a specialist in ethics at the hospital and a Gulf War combat veteran, was charged with overseeing the review of Damian's accusations. In her final report, she concluded that the hospital's (i.e., Sharon's) pat-itself-on-the-back declarations of success were fiction. She added that critical information was being withheld from veterans and VA staff, and that the hospital could be in the grips of what's called "ethical fading." That is what happens when people focus so much on things like profiting (check) and winning (check) that the ethical aspects of their decisions and actions "fade" into the background. Stated differently, since they're always looking for something else, they never see the moral aspects of what they're doing.

Anyway, K.J. and the ethics consult panel made some recommendations when they finished their review, including changes in how the hospital reported its data on appointments. Presumably, they went to Sharon. Not surprisingly, nothing happened. No, let me correct that. Something did happen: K.J. was fired as ethics consultation coordinator, without explanation. But as far as I'm concerned, no explanation was necessary. K.J. was not in the Sharon camp; they'd had some previous run-ins. K.J. said that Sharon's proclamations of success in meeting the WIG goals were false. K.J. said that the hospital needed to change the way it recorded patient appointment data, which would have exposed Sharon's statistics for what they were. K.J. wrote a critical report that was essentially buried (by whom, I wonder).

I rest my case. You decide what was behind K.J.'s firing.

Meanwhile, back to our case...

We still weren't getting much help through traditional channels. Our repeated letters to Secretary Shinseki – which were specific in our criticisms and concerns – got absolutely no traction. Even when Arizona U.S. Rep. Ann Kirkpatrick, who would become one of my biggest supporters, reached out, she was stonewalled. "Mr. Secretary," she wrote on May 13, "I am requesting that you ask for a review of the appropriateness of Ms. Pedene's reassignment. I am also requesting a briefing on the nature of the official review or investigation being conducted on Ms. Pedene."

He replied that there was an "ongoing investigation" being conducted at Phoenix VA, and that it would supposedly be completed by the end of July. "Due to the sensitive employee issues," he continued, "we are not at liberty to discuss the details." He went on to add the hypocritical boiler-plate platitudes: "Please be assured our goal is to create a work environment that is conducive for employees to provide the best care possible to the Veterans we have the privilege to serve."

"Best care possible"? How was that working out so far?

It was becoming more and more obvious that the traditional channels weren't going to work. Personally, I'd reached the point where I felt I could no longer sit back idly while this nightmare was unfolding around me. It had to stop.

The letter Amy and I had written earlier generated some activity, but not enough action. So, I decided to write another one, also anonymous because my case was still ongoing, except this time it would go to the General Accounting Office. While I was banished to the library, I had been watching YouTube videos of the House Veterans Affairs Committee and learned that Debra Draper, who was a director with the GAO's Health Care team and oversaw audits on veteran's care, was hot on VA's trail. I thought maybe, just maybe, reaching out to her office might get someone's attention.

Despite Sharon's stated goal of improving patient access, I wrote on Aug. 11, the hospital's senior leadership in February 2013 directed medical support assistants, or MSAs, to put the scheduling of new patients on hold. The assistants were told to inform new patients they would be placed on an electronic wait list and be called back within a few days to schedule an appointment. It was a lie, and it came straight from the top.

"In fact," I continued in the GAO letter, "from February until May, none of these patients were being placed on the electronic wait list, nor were they being called back and scheduled for new patient appointments. Instead, what was happening is that the new patients who ask for an appointment in their clinic are having their demographic screen printed and placed into a paper pile. The paper pile was then moved between the desk drawers in the Data Management Office and amongst a select few MSAs.

"Additionally, when patients called the VA help line, they were also telling patients they will be placed on an electronic wait list; however, like the clinics, they too were printing the demographic patient screen and sending paper identifiers to a Data Management team where the patient information is being collected...

"No appointments were being scheduled for new patients, contrary to what the Director is telling staff and patients. In fact, the director is saying that new patient requests are on the decline due to our 'winter visitors' leaving."

There you have it. The core of the Wait Time Scandal.

A patient calls in, their information goes onto the computer and is printed out, then is vaporized from the computer by staff at the direction of their higher-ups, and the printouts are stacked and locked away. When an appointment opens months later, the patient gets a call-back, and an appointment goes on the books. With data entered from the original printouts, a new computer file is created showing the appointment was set up within seven to fourteen days of the initial contact, just like Sharon had been saying.

Except it had been months. And from what we were seeing, it was killing patients.

Pauline DeWenter, who handled the wait lists, would call patients for appointments months after they'd initially contacted the hospital – only to be told they had died. The family of one veteran specifically said that he died while waiting for the hospital to contact him for an Urgent Care appointment. There was one Iraq War veteran in Phoenix who suffered from post-traumatic stress disorder. He sent the VA a letter in 2011 saying that his condition was getting so bad it "drives me to consider suicide very seriously on a daily basis." He got no response. On June 30, 2013, he shot himself in the head. He was thirty. In his suicide note, he wrote that "the government had turned around and abandoned me."

This, apparently, is what success seemed to look like to Sharon Helman.

I want to state clearly that none of this was the fault of the MSAs. As I wrote in the Aug. 11 letter, they repeatedly brought their concerns over the appointment scheduling scheme to Health Administration Service (HAS) leadership but received no response or guidance. Not only that, I said, but "HAS staff are being required to fraudulently change appointments while their supervisor watches."

Despite my high hopes for the GAO letter, nothing happened. But the news wasn't all bad.

I found out that Dr. Sam Foote, who I had worked with on the complaints against the hospital's previous leadership, was collecting data on his own. As the director of the Thunderbird VA Health Care Clinic in Phoenix, he had a patient load of about 1,500 veterans. He started asking them how long they'd had to wait for appointments and compared their responses to Sharon's claim that it was fourteen to thirty days. The patients said six to nine months. By late August, he was writing letters of his own to the Office of the Inspector General, and he wasn't doing it anonymously. He was signing every one of them. So, investigators now had someone making the charges on the record. They'd have no choice but to conduct a formal review.

I mean, you'd think so, right?

27

OH, NO, THEY DON'T

But I digress, back on the VA Whistleblower Case…
Stephanie reached out to Rep. Kirkpatrick, who, along with her staff, emerged as real advocates for me, always asking how I was doing and sending their prayers and best wishes. In August, Rep. Kirkpatrick told the Phoenix VA leadership she wanted an update on the status of my case, and further requested that they share results with her.

Nothing.

Here you have a member of Congress, someone who is a member of the House Veterans Affairs Committee and represents Arizona, and VA executives are outright defying her requests. Like Roger said, they think they have been bestowed with some holier-than-thou power that, in their minds, elevated them above everyone – including a member of the U.S. House of Representatives who sat on the Veterans Affairs Committee. Unbelievable.

Roger and I thought hospital leadership were being non-responsive, either because they didn't want to show their hand, or they knew they had a weak case but weren't ready to admit it. Whatever the cause, it didn't stop them from taking another shot at me while they could.

Sharon was having a difficult time finding a qualified replacement for me in public affairs. So, one day, she decided to elevate Shelby Roy, who was my library boss, into the spot. It did not make a bit of sense. Shelby had no practical PR experience. But on the other hand, I could sense she was thinking it could lead to a promotion into the front office. Since ambition was a primary requirement for becoming a member of the executive team, she appeared to have the necessary skillset for public affairs. In something of an ironic twist, she said that since I worked for her, she'd be asking for my support in helping in her "new job."

Really?

I told Stephanie, who was less than happy with the news. "Oh, no, they don't," she said, and she fired off a letter to Susan Bowers of the Veterans Integrated Services Network on Aug. 28 that briefly recounted all of our by-now-familiar complaints, including the fact that we had not been provided results of the AIB hearing in the required time frame, that I was not given the right to know the specific charges against me, and that the 30-day investigation had stretched to nine months. Stephanie then accused the VA of continuing its pattern of harassment with Shelby's proposed detail. She noted that VA had treated me like a "non-entity" and shown me absolutely no professional courtesy, and that the hospital was "trying to make it as uncomfortable as possible to force Ms. Pedene to involuntarily resign or breakdown from the undue stress of the daily uncertainty." The letter was sent to a number of big wigs in Washington, including the Under Secretary for Health, the Office of General Counsel, the Office of Legislative Affairs, and VA Central Office Human Resources.

It worked. Shelby's detail as Public Affairs Officer was immediately halted. That was the good news. Then we got some even better news: The Office of Special Counsel had reviewed our submission for whistleblower reprisal and assigned an investigator to my case.

As the summer came to an end, it was clear that Rep. Kirkpatrick was getting fed up with Lance and Sharon's antics. So, she sent a "suspense" letter from the House Veterans Affairs Committee basically ordering them to turn over specific charges against me no later than Oct. 31. That deadline passed without action (no surprise). Then Lance's office called on Nov. 1 and said he needed an urgent meeting with me that same day. It was short notice, probably by design, and didn't work either for me, as Steven had a medical appointment, or for Stephanie, who lived in Minnesota. So, we gave them a list of other available dates. But rather than reschedule this "urgent" meeting, they decided to mail us the charges instead.

"Mail" being something of a misnomer.

On Nov. 8, UPS rolled up to the front door of our home and unloaded two large boxes that contained nine three-inch binders. They were accompanied by a memo from Lance that said he was demoting me from a GS-13 Public Affairs Officer to a GS-11 Voluntary Service Specialist based on the "misconduct" referenced in a July 19 summary report on the AIB hearing (which we had not seen). My heart sank. It takes years in the federal government to go from grade to grade. The drop to a GS-11 would be a huge setback to my career that I might not ever be able to recover from. I felt that Lance and Sharon were still trying to destroy me professionally.

So, you can imagine my surprise when Roger called and said, "Congratulations."

"They want to demote me," I replied, in tears. "Why are you congratulating me?"

"They wanted to fire you or force you out, and they couldn't do either. Don't worry. This won't stick. We've seen the evidence you received from the FOIA, and they don't have a leg to stand on."

"But –"

"Paula, quit crying and start fighting again." Roger was never one to mince words.

Stephanie and I spoke after Roger's call, and we noticed something that didn't ring quite true. Lance referenced a July 19 AIB summary report which, despite our requests, we'd never been shown because they said it was "pre-decisional." In other words, not final. Except now, it was being used as the basis of a recommendation to demote me. Once again, I didn't know the specific charges, but it sure felt like the summary had in some way been orchestrated to provide an "official" record of charges that we knew were false and could not be substantiated.

I didn't know how right I would be.

28
COUNTERATTACK

If there were any doubts that the AIB conclusions would be rigged against me, they were dispelled in the fourth paragraph of the "pre-decisional" investigation report that Lance was using in his attempt to demote me:

"After careful consideration, the Board decided not to interview the following individuals as it was determined their testimony would not be relevant to the instant case." Nine names followed, all of them submitted by me. So, I was being charged, tried, and judged without being granted the basic right to present my defense. That may be the Sharon and Lance way, but it sure isn't the American way.

The rest of the report was a joke. That's the only way to put it. The Finding of Facts section included:

"On approximately December 4, 2012, the incident witnessed by Mr. Scherpf regarding Ms. Pedene's husband was brought to the attention of Kim Tesh, Privacy and FOIA Officer and it was reported to her as a security/privacy event, and she initiated a privacy ticket and commenced a privacy violation investigation."

No mention that VA had said it was not a security violation, and that there were emails confirming that.

"During the course of the privacy investigation conducted by Ms. Tesh, she found that there was an authorization by a patient to post information on Facebook. Ms. Tesh stated that the veteran didn't sign it; the patient was terminal, and the nurse said that she couldn't sign it; regardless, the picture was posted on Facebook which is a privacy violation in and of itself." Except we had a consent form, signed with an "X," which was a perfectly acceptable form of agreement. If the Board had called the nurse who made the request, this would not be an issue. But it didn't because that would have revealed the truth.

"On Dec. 11, 2012, Ms. Janet Adams, Chief Financial Officer, sent an email to Associate Director Lane Robinson with the subject line of URGENT - Misuse of Appropriate funds." Now, didn't it seem odd to anyone other than me that her "random" audit occurred the day after I was taken out of my job? And it goes without saying that nowhere in the report is there any reference to Lance calling Janet on a Saturday and ordering her to "find something on Paula, and fast."

It went on and on:

Bill's uploading the PowerPoint photos with no reference to him being an authorized VA volunteer or that I had supervised him according to VA rules. They charged he had "at no time" been assigned anywhere but Medical Media, which was a flat-out lie because he'd been approved to support the Public Affairs function. Accusations of financial mismanagement that included expenditures for Parade advertising (a whopping $120!), first-, second-, and third-place ribbons for float winners ($165.89), wooden bookshelves for the Public Affairs office and displays ($812.50), and Parade logo design and letterhead ($710). They identified nineteen purchases that totaled less than $40,000.

Naturally, they neglected to mention that all the expenditures had been approved by my superiors and had been properly vetted.

The AIB built its entire case on "facts" that could be disproven, charges that would not possibly hold up under VA policies and procedures, and testimony from people who either wanted to destroy me or were terrified of their superiors – testimony that my side was not allowed to rebut. So, it was no surprise that the verdict was guilty, guilty, guilty, with this recommendation:

"The nature and number of violations committed by Ms. Pedene demonstrate that she was derelict in discharging her duties as a manager and federal employee. The Director should consider taking appropriate action up to and including removal." Sharon must have been just beside herself. She and Lance had to be happy, too, that the AIB questioned my relationship with Honoring Arizona's Veterans, which was primarily responsible for the Phoenix VA Veterans Day Parade, saying, "The Director may wish to consider looking further into the issue to ensure that there is not a conflict of interest." Explain to me how, as a veteran, volunteering on my own time for a project to support veterans that the hospital had sponsored for years could be construed as a conflict? It made no sense. Except to Lance and Sharon, who allegedly had successfully rigged the investigation to justify my demotion.

After we got the report, Stephanie moved quickly to delay the action to reduce my position to a GS-11. On Nov. 2, 2013, she sent an amendment to the initial whistleblower reprisal complaint with the Office of Special Counsel in which she pretty much dismantled the AIB's conclusions charge by charge, including the proof that Lance and Kim Tesh knew that Bill's help on the PowerPoint did not constitute a security infraction. She did not hold her fire on the board's tactics, either: "Throughout the proceeding of the AIB, it becomes obvious that Ms. Pedene's presentation was secondary and was marginalized. This is apparent by the lack of unbiased questioning in the AIB and the lack of interviewing Ms. Pedene's witnesses, deemed inconsequential to the instant case. In addition, the questions were often leading the witnesses to respond to a conclusion the Board had made. Simply, Ms. Pedene's response was not heard."

"(T)his open-ended 'investigation' into misconduct continued as orchestrated by Mr. Robinson 'behind the scenes' or 'off the record'. It appears that he employed several resources to get enough general 'infractions' to put 'something' together to accuse Ms. Pedene of some kind of 'misconduct.' They all boil down to a VA volunteer who assisted an employee, with a documented visual disability, with VA related work product for public information sharing of a veteran's related activity, specifically, the fourth largest VA Veterans Day Parade in the country (sponsored by the VA). Items purchased by Ms. Pedene to use at work, for work, and to enhance the work product produced by Ms. Pedene as the VA Public Affairs Officer are obvious and typical of such a program."

She went on to accuse Lance, Sharon, and Susan Bowers of actions that were "egregious, abusive, and discriminatory," and charged that leadership had conspired to "neutralize" me. She asked OSC to issue a stay of action preventing my demotion so we could respond to the board's findings. On Dec. 4, 2013, OSC granted it.

As was so often the case throughout this process, the win was short-lived. Not that it wasn't significant, but just that we barely had a chance to enjoy it.

At this point, a year after Lance's infamous Dec. 10, 2012 letter, our medical and legal bills were backing us into a corner. We were having to spend way more money than we were taking in, and there wasn't a whole lot of sunshine on the horizon. We'd filed a case with the Equal Opportunity Employment Commission, but that wouldn't reach a court for three years. And while the OSC case was progressing, it was slow going. We went over our finances almost daily, cutting here, saving there, sacrificing where we could, but eventually, Bill and I had to face a cold, hard fact: We were quickly running out of money. Our only option, it seemed, was to agree to a financial settlement with VA and put an end to this agony.

Roger would hear no such thing.

"I'm ready to give up," I told him one day.

"Don't do it."

"I don't really have a choice."

"Yes, you do. If you give up, they win."

"They're winning anyway."

"No, they're not. But if you let them, they won't stop with you. They'll come after anyone who gets in their way. They won't stop until they've crushed them, too. And sooner or later, nobody will stand up to them, and they will have full rein to do whatever they want, to whoever they want, with no fear of any consequences."

I told him I wasn't in this to be martyr. He told me I wasn't a martyr. I was a fighter. "So go fight."

I promised I would. But as it turned out, it wasn't the fight I'd planned on fighting.

152

29
A DILEMMA

As I said earlier, Dr. Sam Foote, who was director of the Thunderbird VA Health Care Clinic in Phoenix, had begun writing letters to the Veterans Affairs Department's Office of the Inspector General, raising issues about patient waits and delays in getting care. By December 2013, he'd sent three letters, copying members of the Arizona congressional delegation among others on each of them. The OIG came to Phoenix to investigate, but the hospital leadership apparently did what it did best – dodging, weaving, rebutting, lying, and denying. Despite Sam's best efforts to expose what was going on, nothing happened.

Sam is one of my favorite people. He's a larger-than-life guy, a UCLA grad who grew up in Los Angeles, and a terrific doctor whose specialty is internal medicine. To call him no-nonsense would be an understatement. Sam did not suffer fools gladly, and when he came across a fool, well, the fool suffered. That's who Sam is. He is passionate about our veterans, and he knew Sharon was cooking the books to make her access numbers look good.

While he never wanted the attention that would later follow him as the public face of the wait list whistleblowing, Sam felt like he had to do something about the situation at the hospital. Let me tell you, when Sam is on a mission, it's wise to support him or get out of his way.

Oddly, Lance seemed obsessed with Sam. Or maybe terrified is a better way to put it. I remember a meeting we had on Sept. 24, 2012. After Dr. Darren Deering, the hospital's Chief of Staff, had informed him I was having conversations with Sam on weekends, Lance cornered me in my office for the third degree. He wanted to know about my relationship with Sam and why I was talking to him. At the time, I thought Lance was just being more curious and suspicious than anything else. But when I told him Sam had blown the whistle on the previous leadership, his trademark hostility kicked in. He asked me again about Sam's role in the ousting of Reyes and Beam, and I told him again. He got all blustery and huffy. "I am going to find out about this Foote fellow."

Except he already knew. He'd previously been briefed about Sam, about me, and about what we'd done to remove the prior leadership by the VISN leaders who hired him. Looking back, this was probably Lance on a fact-finding expedition, trying to see what I knew, if he could find something to use against me, and assessing whether Sam and I were planning to come after him and Sharon. We weren't, at least we weren't at that time.

By this time, though, I wasn't the only one facing reprisal.

Lance and Sharon were also gunning for Sam. He faced things like job reprisals, leave denials, false accusations, and removal of authority – the little things federal managers can use to make someone miserable and force them out. While I don't want to downplay or dismiss their attacks on him – there is no excuse or justification – I can't help but be struck by the fact that they didn't torment him to the degree they tormented me. I'm not interested in playing the gender card here but come on. They didn't want to mess too badly with a man (one they probably knew they shouldn't cross) but threw everything at me, a legally blind female veteran, and sat back waiting to see what stuck. I don't think it's a stretch to call them predators who preyed on those they believed were weak in order to make their lives better.

By the end of 2013, it didn't matter what they tried to do to Sam. He decided to retire and was going to do whatever it took to get the Wait Time Scandal out of the dark corners of the hospital and into the public spotlight. You've heard of archangels, rights? They safeguard humanity and protect mankind. They find solutions to human problems. They are the chief and higher messengers. Sam would be all of that for the veterans. And he wanted my help.

Boy, talk about a dilemma.

Thanks to Lance and Sharon, my life had become a living hell because I'd joined with Sam in the case against the previous leadership. Now, with my family unraveling, our bills stacking higher and higher, and our financial resources falling lower and lower, I had to make a decision: either double down on the fight and face the likelihood that hospital management would continue to crush opposing voices like mine and escalate its war of attrition against me, or take a pass, let Sam more or less go it alone, and hopefully avoid any further collateral damage to my family and career.

On the one hand, it seemed pretty simple. Even though there were moments for optimism, Steven's bipolar disorder still wasn't under control, and treatments and therapies were expensive. Robert had moved to Flagstaff with his girlfriend, and they had a falling out – a really bad breakup that rattled him a lot – so he came home in rough shape. But for all he was dealing with, after he walked in the front door and told us what had happened to him, he said, "I'm sorry, Mom, for leaving. I walked out on you."

"You didn't walk on me," I said. "You didn't walk out on any of us. Why do you say that?"

"I saw everything you were going through and all the things those people were doing to you, and all the stuff with Steven. I saw what it was doing to you. I thought things might be a little easier for you if I wasn't around."

I tried to hold back the tears. "That isn't true."

"If I wasn't around, you wouldn't have to worry about me, too. You could stay focused on what was important."

"There's nothing more important to me than you and Steven and your father."

"I know, but when I saw the pressure you were under and what it was doing to you, I just thought it would be better for you if I left." I couldn't hold back the tears anymore. He added, "I feel like I ran when you needed me most."

The mother's hardships, visited on the son. It absolutely crushed me.

This was all taking a toll on Bill, too. I was coming apart, and he had a front-row seat. I believe he felt I was doing the right thing by fighting, but I also think he was wondering whether doing what was right was wrong for me. He knew me better than anyone. He knew I just wanted to do what was best for our veterans. He often talked about how I believed in the basic goodness of people. Yet here we were, trying to do good, forced to fight bad people whose only job in life was my destruction. I once asked Bill how worried he was about all this. He laughed. "I only think about it at seven in the morning. And eight. And nine and ten and eleven…"

So, from the family standpoint, it was a no-brainer. Don't jump into another battle on another front.

But I also kept coming back to something Roger had said. He told me this fight was not me against the VA. It was about one person against the institutional evil that Lance and Sharon seemed to represent. There was a time when I would have thought that was hyperbole, but the VA had become a castle of self-preservation that was built to protect its own and their interests, and critics and questioners were not allowed in.

For example, a department employee in Puerto Rico was the driver in an armed robbery and was arrested. In a normal world, she would have been fired. But VA world is not a normal world. The robbery was at three in the morning, and a department spokesman suggested that it was okay for employees to participate in a crime if was on their own time. David Shulkin, who was then an undersecretary at the agency, said, "There was never any indication that the employee posed a risk to Veterans or VA property." Forget right and wrong, or public safety, or the fact that the guy she was with robbed a couple at gunpoint. She was fired and jailed but then later reinstated at the VA – with back pay.

At the VA hospital in Alexandria, Louisiana, an employee had a confrontation with a 70-year-old veteran and beat him to death. The local coroner said the victim died of blunt force trauma to the head. Witnesses told investigators they saw the man hitting the patient. The VA conducted an internal investigation and concluded the death was accidental – Accidental! – and allowed the employee to keep treating patients. He even got a week of paid leave to recover from the fight. He remained on the payroll for years. Eventually, Louisiana prosecutors charged him with murder – "He did…kill a human being," they wrote – and bond was set at $250,000. But the charge was dropped to manslaughter because VA's lack of disciplinary action was seen as indicating the agency did not see it as the truly atrocious crime that it was.

So, when Roger talked about institutional evil, it was no exaggeration.

I was in a damned if you do, damned if you don't scenario. Even so, it was no time to wring my hands. I had to make a call, and I wasn't going to do it alone.

One night, shortly after Sam had approached me, we all sat around the table – Bill, Steven, Robert, and me. I explained to them about the two lists and how we had seen the evidence that Sharon was manipulating the data to show that wait times were declining rather than growing, and that veterans were dying as a result. I told them I could help Sam and do it anonymously, behind the scenes. The boys thought that was wishful thinking and said they'd probably come after me anyway, and that as bad as things were, they'd just get worse.

I could not disagree. With that, it felt like a decision had been made. Then the tide turned unexpectedly.

"No," Robert said. We all looked at him, puzzled. "VA is the government. They have all this power. And they're using it against you. They're afraid of one little person because you scare them. They don't have the right to do that."

"They don't," Steven said.

I looked at Bill, and there was so much pride in his eyes and mine. These kids, who had sacrificed and suffered so much, had just given their mom permission to find her inner David. The time had come at long last to slay the bureaucratic Goliath.

30
A Mighty Collaboration Is Born

You don't mess with Eric Hannel. It's just a really bad idea. A combat veteran and ex-Marine who got out of the Corps in 2006, he was in Pensacola, Florida working as military liaison in the U.S. House of Representatives. Jeff Miller's local office. When the Republicans took over the House in 2010, Congressman Miller asked Eric to come to Washington. In no uncertain terms (an Eric specialty), he said there was no way he was leaving Pensacola. Then the congressman asked again. This time, he told *The Hill*, he said yes. "I knew I was pretty fortunate to be asked twice and decided that this is where I'm supposed to be."

In 2011, he became the staff director for the House Committee on Veterans Affairs Subcommittee on Oversight and Investigation. Before that, he worked as a security specialist with the Federal Emergency Management Agency, which was part of the Department of Homeland Security. At DHS, he won praise for a probe that led to the first-ever prosecution of fraud in the department's history.

When Eric was with FEMA, one of his responsibilities was to support the agency's disaster relief efforts. As part of that, he worked days, nights, and weekends to go after scammers who were trying to illegally profit from federal assistance. He tracked down people who had sold the contents of their temporary government-supplied trailers, or even the trailers themselves. He discovered trailers that were being used by drug dealers and shut them down. He uncovered people who were receiving federal aid even though they were ineligible, such as convicts, bail jumpers, and scam artists who followed disaster recovery efforts just so they could get (steal) federal money from each one. He once caught someone who claimed federal aid in order to get cash to repair her various rental properties, none of which had been damaged by disasters. He was a dogged investigator with a tremendous sense of justice who believed that wrongdoing had no place in this world. If you were doing wrong, Eric was not the guy you wanted on your tail. As I said, you don't mess with him.

But rousting drug dealers, scammers, crooks, and cheats was easy compared to dealing with the sharks at VA.

Eric believed deep down that something was going on with the wait lists. He knew about William Schoenhard's April 26, 2010 memo that, while trying to correct leadership issues on the wait lists, actually became a guideline for how to game the system. He understood the appointment process and thought it just wasn't possible for hospitals like ours to see veterans within a 14-day window. Doctors and nurses would be off duty, ill, or on vacation. Computers would go down, and back-up systems would kick in. Schedules would get mixed up. Then, of course, there was the fact that the patient enrollments were consistently rising at a time when, at least in Phoenix, we were seeing an exodus of health care professionals, many of whom told me it was due to poor

160

leadership. Add all that up, and you don't get improved access to care. You get longer waits.

Eric wasn't buying any of the "wait-time improvements" nonsense. He'd made numerous requests for information from the VA but got nothing in return. He sent emails to the media starting in 2013. They said his accusations were just that – accusations, based on his opinions – and that they needed proof, as in documents, rather than anecdotes. But he couldn't get subpoenas, his FOIA requests were routinely ignored, no one would speak on the record, and when he did get any kind of paperwork, most of the content was redacted. In the unlikely event that the media would follow up on one of his tirades, the hospital leadership would bring out four or five veterans who repeated the VA line that care was great, access was great, and everything was hunky dory. With nothing to go on, the reporters would return to their newsroom empty-handed, and the story would return to the shadows.

None of this sat well with Eric, who once called the VA a "self-licking ice cream cone" and was the first to admit that he didn't run very well on idle. I mean, here was a guy who said his top priority as Rep. Miller's staff aide was to "hold the Veterans Affairs Department accountable, to combat its corporate culture, and to ensure the voice of truth is heard without deference to partisan politics, bureaucracy or careerists." Those were exactly the problems we were fighting in Phoenix, and he was fighting all over the country. Every time he turned around, no matter what he did, he was treated the same way federal investigators and members of Congress were being treated: with callous indifference.

All he needed were two things: someone willing to speak up publicly, and evidence that veterans were being forced to wait for their care. He certainly wasn't getting the intel from the VA. I had reached out to try to get him what he needed and sent several staff to him to share what evidence they had. It helped some, but it wasn't the brass ring we needed. Then I hooked him up with Sam Foote.

Prior to announcing his retirement in December 2013, Sam told me he could see that we weren't going to get anywhere with his letters to the VA Office of Inspector General or my anonymous letters and attempts to provide VA investigators with our letters and evidence. That's when he said he was going to leave the job early so he could "blow this whole thing wide open."

I said, "Sam, whatever I can do to help you, I will. We have to stop this evil. Their lies, their falsehoods, them hurting our patients, and decimating morale, it just all has to stop."

We teamed up immediately.

We agreed that the first line of attack would be to feed the story to the *Arizona Republic*. It made sense. The paper had published Dennis Wagner's March 2013 article about me being demoted after testifying against the previous leadership, so Dennis was not blind to the fact that something wasn't quite right at the hospital. But I knew Sam would need some media training prior to meeting with Dennis and others at the paper. I thought about who the best person would be to coach him, and it dawned on me it would be Rick Romley, who had dealt with all kinds of media when prosecuting some horrific scandals in Arizona. I contacted Rick, and he agreed, as he was already livid at VA for what they were doing to me and for trying to kill the Parade.

Rick prepped Sam for a sit-down. Although Sam had done some media training through programs I'd offered as public affairs officer, getting schooled by Rick was like getting a master class in dealing with the press. He knew how Sam could discuss and leverage the issues at the hospital without violating any laws.

Rick also showed Sam the importance of being short and to the point, instructed him on evidence-sharing case law, and helped him use analogies to make a point. These were two brilliant men, and I think they enjoyed the back and forth that comes with crafting a media strategy. Everybody thought we were on our way.

The *Republic*, however, didn't think we had the evidence it needed to climb on board.

When Sam met with Dennis and his editors, there was no doubt the paper was interested in the story. The problem was, they needed a verified second source. I get that. Sam was forceful and persuasive, but he had an opinion (a strong one) and the absolute knowledge that what he was saying was true (which it was). Let's face it, though. This was a hot-button story. The *Republic* was not about to go out on that particular limb without factual backup, even in an age where content goes unsourced every minute of every day on the Internet. They wanted a second source, and I respect them for that, but finding one who would go on the record posed a very real threat of violating patient privacy. For all his righteous outrage, Sam wasn't going to do that.

When we talked about next steps, I told Sam that our best shot now was to get evidence to the House Veterans Affairs Committee. Then, if they made it public in any way, the media would have a second source – this one from Congress. I told him about Eric. A mighty collaboration was born.

Sam, being the ever-faithful public servant, wanted to give Phoenix VA one more chance before ringing the congressional bell. So, on Feb. 2, he wrote a final letter to the Office of the Inspector General Hotline, which considers complaints against the department. This time, though, he wrote it as a retired VA physician and pulled no punches. He copied John S. Leonardo, the U.S. attorney for Arizona, Sen. John McCain, and Reps. Miller

163

and Kirkpatrick. Rather than summarize what he said, I'll just put it out there for you to read for yourself:

"I am writing this letter to you in follow-up to the letter that was received by you on October 22, 2013. In that letter, I alleged that the Phoenix VA was currently suffering from gross mismanagement of VA resources, criminal misconduct by VA senior leadership, and that their actions have created systematic patient safety issues and possible wrongful deaths, which I think is an abuse of their authority.

"Since that time, I have forwarded to you information regarding twenty-two people who were placed on the electronic waiting list and died before getting appointments and another eighteen patients who suffered the same fate. We have informed you that we have the names of those individuals, but you have yet to request that we send them to you.

"Agents from the San Diego VA Health and Safety IG (*inspector general*) came out (*to Phoenix*) in mid-December 2013 and confirmed several of the allegations that I have made, yet Director Helman is still running our VA, and patients are still dying. How can that be three months after I first notified you of the problems here? ...(T)his is a medical center that is badly broken and needs to be fixed as quickly as possible! Ms. Helman and her fellow Pentad and HAS (*Health Administration Service*) criminal conspirators have been running multiple scams."

He didn't stop there, laying out five of those scams, the first two of which related directly to the wait lists:

"**Scam 1**: The electronic waiting list. About 5,500 patients affected with twenty-two dead.

The VA had been using a schedule system called desired date, but there was so much wide-spread fraud, they changed to creation date. Example: You come in and request an appt. The soonest I can give you is 291 days out. So, do you want that one sir? If we get a cancellation, we will move you up. You agree, and I click off desired date 291 days from now so the computer then shows that you did not have to wait any time at all for this appointment.

"To put a stop to this, they started counting time from the creation date which is the date the employee entered the (request into the) computer to make the appointment, and the clock starts from there. This would expose the Phoenix VA for what it really is, so Brad Curry (*Chief of Phoenix HSA*) and the Pentad violated HIPPA and internal VA policy by having the clerks do a screen capture and then printing it out on the clinic printer, then clearing the screen (thus removing the information from the system). They would then collect the printouts and take them to HAS upstairs. There the patients would be put on the electronic list and then the only record of the visit, the printout, would be shredded. They were caught doing this, so they improved the sophistication of the plan by simply printing these to a dedicated printer in HAS office upstairs.

"**Scam 2:** Schedule an appointment consult. About 5000 patients affected, eighteen dead.

They had the ED (*Emergency Department*) docs along with the inpatient docs and the inpatient social workers using these. The staff thought that if they requested an appointment in three days or a week, they would get one. I had an out-of-control Diabetic patient, new onset with an ED doc request for one week. My MAA (*medical administrative assistant*) found him in a batch of these FOUR MONTHS LATER. We think they completely ignored this list in August and September because they were falsifying vesting visits. We know they did not look at these for two months and severed the link to the printer in HAS so that they would not print out and bother them. This is the time frame where one poor patient became a victim and why it took them two months to answer his consult, about a week after he died. His daughter-in-law is furious over this."

He concluded, "I am not a lawyer, but I would think that deliberately delaying patient care resulting in the death of a patient while trying to obtain a bonus would meet the AZ statute of negligent homicide."

Negligent homicide.

Strong accusations and harsh words, but they got the attention of someone who would eventually serve as our second source and bring down the house of cards that Sharon and Lance had so cruelly constructed.

31
VETERANS DAY

Veterans finally got their day on April 9, 2014.

Throughout March, Sam had continued to work with the *Arizona Republic* and various other media outlets, still trying to make the Wait Time Scandal public, but the same obstacles remained. Media needed names of the forty veterans whose deaths Sam had referenced in his February letter to VA. If he shared them, it would mean compromising the personally identifiable information on a patient. At no time did we consider that. Despite what the yahoos at the hospital were doing, we knew the bottom line of our job was to protect patients, and that included protecting their information. Meanwhile, the *Republic* was filing information requests with VA and (in typical fashion) was getting nothing in return.

At our end, I was talking with Sam and giving him suggestions. He used a lot of my recommendations – getting with Rick on media prep, working with Jeff Miller's team on Oversight and Investigations, writing more letters, talking to other reporters. But I suspected that he had something else, something big, in the works. As I've said, Sam is brilliant and a force of nature. In addition to all the advice he was getting, he told me he had one big idea of his own. When I asked him to share it, he politely declined out of concern for my job security. "Paula, I'm working on it, and this is going to come to light." Sam was clearly adding to the strategy we had put in place, and that was good enough for me.

Meanwhile, I spoke routinely with Eric Hannel and others, keeping them in the loop. As he kept his boss, Rep. Jeff Miller, who chaired the Veterans Affairs Committee, in the loop as well, we could all sense that the congressman was growing more furious and frustrated day by day. So, with Sam feeding information to the media, and me making sure Eric (and, by extension, Rep. Miller and others) were up to speed, the pieces were in place.

But we still didn't have that verified second source the media needed, and we couldn't share what evidence we had with them. Without that, the story was going nowhere.

All that changed on April 9.

Rep. Miller was chairing a hearing that was aptly titled, "A Continued Assessment of Delays in VA Medical Care and Preventable Deaths." It was no doubt a reflection of his anger over what was happening to veterans in Phoenix. I was sitting in my chair in the library, watching the hearing. People had told me that Sharon, Lance, and their allies were watching it in her conference room. While I was glued to the proceedings, staff told me that the leadership was bantering with each other and carrying on, acting aloof and seeing Congress as mere subjects and minor irritants. The hearing was little more than background noise to them.

About an hour and a half into the session, Congressman Miller personally took his time in the "pulpit" as Chair and began questioning Dr. Thomas Lynch, the Assistant Deputy

Undersecretary for Clinical Operations for Health for the Department of Veterans Affairs. He told Lynch the topic was "unofficial wait lists at the Phoenix VA." As I said earlier, Dr. Lynch seemed unfazed by the title.

Rep. Miller said that committee investigators – that is, Eric and his team – had gathered evidence that Phoenix VA was keeping two sets of records in order to conceal patient wait times. "It appears as though there could be as many as forty veterans whose deaths could be related to delays in care," he said. The room fell silent. It was as if no one dared to take a breath. "Were you made aware of these official lists?" A few seconds passed.

Finally, Dr. Lynch responded, "Mr. Chairman, I was not." He then asked for more information from the investigative staffers.

Rep. Miller wasn't satisfied. He bored in. "So, your people had two lists, and they even kept it from your knowledge?" It was as much a statement as it was a question, but he made his point. With his words, the secret was no longer a secret, and the scandal had been exposed! Light flashes from photographers lit up Dr. Lynch's face while TV cameras lingered on Rep. Miller as he gaveled the hearing back to order. The sight felt unreal.

I couldn't believe it. I put my hands over my mouth, ecstatic. Mark, my supervisor looked at me strangely, as if he wasn't quite sure what had just happened. But I was. The list of veterans who had died became public thanks to Congressman Miller. The media had the evidence it needed, and a second source in Rep. Miller, who had issued a protective order to preserve critical records at the hospital (no doubt to prevent them from being shredded) and released the list as an "official disclosure" at the hearing.

All we could do was sit back and see what the response was. It was explosive.

The *Arizona Republic* rushed to publish a lengthy story on its website that was headlined, "Deaths at Phoenix VA hospital may be tied to delayed care." One paragraph said whistleblowers charged that "Arizona VA executives collect bonuses for reducing patient wait times, yet purported successes stem from manipulation of data instead of improved service to our veterans."

Sharon's comment in the article was weak, the kind of non-denial denial that was designed to avoid the issue and the question of blame: "We take seriously any issue that occurs in our medical center and outpatient clinics. Therefore, we have asked for an external review by the VA Office of the Inspector General. If the OIG finds areas that need to be improved, we will swiftly address them, as our goal is to provide the best care possible to our veterans." But make no mistake, she was finally starting to sweat. We were told later she walked as briskly as possible through the hospital (given her short skirt) after the hearing, the click-click-click of her high heels reverberating in the hallways. She talked to Lance and some of the people in Health Administrative Service, trying to get a handle on the damage and how to control it. No matter. Every public comment she'd make in the coming days would do little more than spray gasoline on a fire that was burning out of control.

On April 23, CNN went on the air with a nearly eight-minute story. We knew it was coming. This was Sam's "additional strategy," and he executed it perfectly. We organized a watch party at our home. The report was devastating.

Anderson Cooper stared into the camera on the CNN set in New York. His face was darkened by a sense of anger. He spoke deliberately and forcefully:

"Our CNN 360 exclusive tonight is on how veterans are dying while they wait for medical care at VA hospitals...We've uncovered how far one VA hospital went to hide its outrageously long wait times. Forty veterans died while waiting for care, and although that would be shocking enough, in 'Keeping Them

Honest,' there's more. A doctor, who recently left the hospital, said managers were keeping two waiting lists – a sham list that made the hospital look like a model of efficiency and a secret list that showed the hospital's deadly reality. CNN's Drew Griffin has more…"

You could have heard a pin drop in our home. By the way, we found out later that the actual number of veterans who died was 293.

Sam Foote, who watched with us, was on camera. He told Drew the number of deaths in Phoenix was likely higher than the forty that had already been revealed, and went on to explain how the secret wait lists worked:

"The only record that you have ever been here requesting care was on that secret list. And they wouldn't take you off that secret list until you had an appointment time that was less than fourteen days, so it would give the appearance that they were improving greatly the waiting times, when in reality it had been six, nine, in some cases twenty-one months."

He went on to say that if a patient died waiting for an appointment, "they could just remove you from that list, and there's no record that you ever came to the VA and presented for care."

"Pretty convenient," Drew said.

"Pretty sad," Sam replied.

The broadcast also included emails that showed hospital leadership, including Sharon, "knew about the actual wait times, knew about the off-the-books list, and defended its use to her staff." Drew continued, "Which makes this statement from Helman all the more strange." Her comment read, "It is disheartening to hear allegations about Veterans' care being compromised, and we are open to any collaborative discussion that assists in our goal to continually improve patient care." Drew characterized that response as "stunning." Sam agreed, saying that the secret lists were part of a plan that included the top five leaders at the hospital. "Basically," Drew said, "you have medical directors cooking the books."

"Correct," Sam said.

As for me, Sharon professing concern for the welfare of veterans was a little like a cat talking about the welfare of mice.

Three weeks after Congressman Miller's hearing, media all over the world were still reporting about the secret lists. On the VA front, someone higher up finally got to Sharon and advised her that the denials weren't working. Things were spinning out of control. I have to admit, it was fascinating to watch. Sam continued to stay in touch with Drew Griffin at CNN, feeding him ways to stealthily – but appropriately – find ways to get Sharon on camera. We laughed so hard the day Sam told him she'd stopped parking her car in her regular area and had begun hunkering down in a space outside the Emergency Department where VA police were patrolling. If she thought it was a safe haven, boy was she wrong. One day she came out, and there was Drew and his camera crew, and they were shouting questions at her, and she looked absolutely deer-in-the-headlights dazed. All she could do was climb into her blue Mercedes coup and speed off.

I'm not sure who told her, after that fiasco, it would be a good idea to sit down with Drew for an interview. Even with all the media reports and hearings, I don't think these poor suckers had any idea all the evidence would come right back around and point to leadership. Perhaps still feeling above it all, I suppose they thought they had the power to turn a negative into a positive. So, Sharon, along with Dr. Darren Deering, the hospital chief of staff, faced off with Drew. It wasn't a total disaster. Just a total fabrication. And no contest.

In that April 30 interview, Sharon said, "When we heard about this during the House Veterans Affairs Committee hearing, it is the first time we have heard about those allegations, and that is why we've asked the Office of Inspector General to come in and do a thorough and impartial review."

Drew looked straight at her and said, "That is an odd statement." He reminded her that as early as the previous fall, OIG had already been looking into the allegations of a secret waiting list and veterans' deaths. Sharon acknowledged she had been questioned at that time but didn't know what the questioning was about. "They don't tell us what the allegations are surrounding their investigation." Really? Sharon knew that knowledge was power, and she knew everything. Drew then cited multiple sources saying Sharon and Darren were aware of the scheduling manipulation because "it was their plan." The two of them tag-teamed on the answer.

Sharon: "Any concerns that staff have, I share in those same concerns."

Deering: "We have never instructed our staff to create a secret list, to maintain a secret list, to shred a secret list. That has never come from our office as far as instruction to our staff."

Sharon: "It's never come from me. As a leader of this organization, I'm going to continue to provide the best health care that these veterans deserve and earned."

I could see that both of them were flustered, which is where we wanted them to be. It was time for the tables to turn, and for them to be on the hot seat, under investigation, just as so many of us had been.

While watching it, I could not understand how they could lie so brazenly. So many staff knew about the two lists, and they also knew Sharon was behind them. She wanted to move up in the VA hierarchy and allegedly created a performance scheme to help her get there. It wasn't a secret to any of us. But now, with the accusation that forty veterans had died, and their names as part of the record, you would think that Sharon would have seen the handwriting on the wall. But then again, this is Sharon we're talking about. She thought she was invincible. To her, this may have been little more than a minor speed bump. You could even argue that when a person gets so good at lying, what's demonstrably false becomes true in their own mind.

On the other hand, maybe someone whispered in her ear that it was time to find legal representation.

In the CNN interview, when Drew asked her about the wait list charges, Sharon kept referring to the OIG investigation. "Those are the allegations that we've asked the inspector general to review," she said at one point.

"But I assume those are the allegations that you two would have direct knowledge of," Drew responded.

"Again, those allegations are the ones that the Office of Inspector General is reviewing right now."

I'm not an attorney, and I don't presume to know what advice Sharon was getting, or from whom, but falling back on that statement, which she kept repeating, sure sounded like the words of someone who had lawyered up and been advised accordingly. She was more than willing to wait it out (no pun intended), just as she'd done while still managing to climb up so many rungs on her career ladder. After all, she may have rigged the investigative process before. Who was to say she couldn't do it again?

32

THE HAMMERS FALL

After the bomb dropped on April 9, the heat was on Sharon. She had weaseled her way out of the letters I'd written, dodged investigators, and seemed to rig the process to protect her and Lance. But this time was different. She wasn't tackling internal policies and procedures she could easily manipulate or brushing off charges from anonymous accusers. She was facing concrete, substantive, and – according to Sam – criminal allegations. But maybe even worse than that, at least for her, she was facing the *Republic*'s Dennis Wagner, who was clearly on a mission.

Her first face-to-face interview with Dennis was scheduled for May 1 and followed three weeks of bad news for Sharon, her team, and the Phoenix VA. Reports from publications ranging from the *Republic* to *The Wall Street Journal* put the hospital and Sharon's leadership in an increasingly harsh glare. On April 23, Arizona Sens. John McCain and Jeff Flake asked for Senate hearings and an inquiry into the charges. Of course, I had Sam get in touch with both of their Veterans liaisons, so we could ensure that the truth would come out. Though the senators had been somewhat lackadaisical up to that point, they were now ready to fully engage. By the end of April, three members of the U.S. House, headed by my congressman, Arizona Rep. David Schweikert, demanded the resignation or removal of Sharon and her confederates. President Obama called for an investigation and would later send a White House deputy chief of staff to Phoenix to meet with hospital leaders.

But VA in Washington inexplicably continued to bury its head in the sand.

Dr. Robert Petzel, the Undersecretary for Health who oversaw the Veterans Health Administration, testified before a Senate Committee on April 30, saying that "to date, we have found no evidence of a secret list. We have found no patients who have died because they have been on a wait list."

No evidence? What about the forty names that were made public at Congressman Miller's hearing? What about the on-the-record statements of people who had first-hand knowledge of the scheme? We also knew that Petzel received and read every single letter we sent him about the issues in Phoenix because my representative had sent them via "read receipt," and Petzel was often the first to open them. His role in the cover-up was as significant as it was distasteful.

But none of us were really surprised by his performance on April 30. It was common knowledge that Sharon was in some way being protected by the VA higher-ups, and inside the hospital we all thought Petzel had been providing her cover. His comments before the Senate committee sent a clear message: The department was hunkering down, supporting Sharon, and sticking to the same kind of deceptive script that had served it well over the years. There was little reason to believe that Sharon would stray from the agency line with Dennis, even under what would likely be tough questioning.

Except the interview never happened.

On May 1, 2014, the day after Petzel's "see no evil" testimony and the same day Sharon was supposed to sit down with Dennis, she canceled at the last minute. Why? She, Lance, and Brad Curry, the head of Health Administration Service, were put on administrative leave by VA Secretary Eric Shinseki, who said, "We believe it is important to allow an independent, objective review to proceed…These allegations, if true, are absolutely unacceptable, and if the Inspector General's investigation substantiates these claims, swift and appropriate action will be taken." After dragging its feet for months, the department had finally acknowledged something was rotten in Phoenix, leadership was involved, and action had to be taken.

I imagine that somewhere inside of VA, there was a hope that placing Sharon, Lance, and Brad on leave would somehow reduce the pressure on the hospital. Sorry, but that ship had sailed. The editorials and bad stories just kept cascading down, and the toll extended far beyond the Phoenix VA leadership. During Petzel's testimony, we could all see the look of disdain on Secretary Shinseki's face. So, it wasn't surprising that in mid-May, Dr. Petzel resigned – weeks after his indefensible remarks to the Senate committee. Coincidence? Maybe, maybe not. I do know that before the resignation, Sen. Flake had told Shinseki that Petzel appeared to be "completely tone deaf" to the scandal in Phoenix, and in a May 19 editorial, the *Republic* stated that Petzel's resignation "takes no heat" off the secretary.

That editorial proved to be prophetic.

On May 30, Eric Shinseki resigned. In announcing the decision, President Obama said the secretary told him VA needed "new leadership" to cope with the unfolding scandal and did not want to be a "distraction." Shinseki apologized to Congress and to America's veterans but said, "This situation can be fixed."

I respect Gen. Shinseki. I think he's an honorable man and a caring individual who seemed to be kept in the dark about what was going on in Phoenix and in other VA hospitals throughout the country. He was a victim of people, in and out of Washington, who shielded him from the truth for their own purposes. We'd sent him letters, but most got minimal to no response, and I believe it's because the staff buried our concerns. He took the fall because someone had to, and he was at the top of the pyramid. That's how politics works.

But did I agree that the situation could be fixed?

Let's just say that time would make the final judgment on that.

As all of this was unfolding, I had been calling and texting Dennis routinely, serving as an off-the-record source for background information. It was a risky game, and I was gambling with my career. If Lance and Sharon got so much as an inkling I was talking to the press, they could write me up for insubordination (the gag order, remember?), and that would be the last straw. While it was a victory for the veterans when those two were put on leave, it didn't make me any less anxious. You know how crime bosses can still rule over their organizations when they're in prison? I was pretty sure Lance and Sharon could still run the show even though they were not in their offices.

But I continued to work with Dennis anyway, providing him with information that had to have saved him hours of research. I also persuaded members of the hospital staff to talk with him.

Although no one was eager to risk their job, they knew that Dennis had written the March 2013 story about me, and I assured them he was an honest reporter. One of them who spoke to Dennis was Dr. Kate Mitchell. She had sixteen years with the hospital as a nurse, a supervising physician in the emergency room, and as a medical director overseeing a program that transitioned veterans of the Iran and Afghanistan wars. She had asked me early on what I thought about Dennis and if she could trust him. I told her she could, but I didn't know what information she planned to share with him. On May 2, her story broke, headlined "Second VA doctor blows whistle on patient-care failures." It included this quote from Kate: "I spent my whole professional life wanting to be a VA nurse, and then a VA physician. ...(But) the insanity in the system right now needs to stop, and whatever I can do to accomplish that, I will."

Another was Pauline DeWenter, our vanpool driver who was in charge of the electronic waiting lists. Initially, she was afraid to talk to anyone but CNN, but I told her that it was also important for our Phoenix community to have Dennis cover the story locally as well. She agreed and met with him at our home. His article was first published June 23, headlined "New whistle-blower says Phoenix VA concealed deaths." This was a key paragraph:

"DeWenter said a supervisor, who she declined to name, ordered her to gather new-patient appointment requests week after week and place them in her desk drawer. She estimated that more than 1,000 veterans were sidetracked onto that 'secret list' — ignored for weeks or months because they couldn't be scheduled within a 14-day goal set for wait times by VA administrators." She also said that Sharon had warned employees in a meeting to follow her orders in the effort to reduce wait times, threatening to "buy you a pass" on the bus out of the VA if they didn't.

The next day, CNN aired an interview with Pauline in which she said someone was trying to hide the real number of veterans who died waiting for care by going on the computer and changing someone who was identified to saying they were not dead. She said she was told to take new requests from veterans seeking care and hide them in a desk drawer. Those requests, she said, constituted the secret lists. "It's beyond horrible," she said. Beyond that, even with Sam Foote's disclosures to the Office of Inspector General, she said leadership kept saying, "'Oh, we passed everything; we're not doing anything wrong.' And I'm like, we're not doing anything wrong, and people are still dying?'"

I also arranged for Dennis to interview K.J. Sloan. That story ran on June 24, discussing her firing over the ethics report. In it, Dennis pointed out that while she had never been told explicitly why she was fired, she believed it was in retaliation for her criticism. "That was the reason, absolutely," she told him. "It was quite clear to me I had said what was not to be said. And, believe me, I tried to be politically correct because it's very dangerous there.'

The wins were starting to add up. At last, the light I was seeing at the end of the tunnel wasn't a train bearing down on me.

By this time, the leadership had followed through on its plan to relocate the library from the third floor to the basement to make room for a call center. The library staff, the hospital staff, and the patients were not happy about the move. It meant less space for operations, no windows, and terrible cell phone reception. Beyond that, it would be out of the way for staff who needed to gather materials for their research studies and too far away for patients who wanted to use its resources. That probably bothered me as much as anything. Patients loved to take walks, get out of their rooms, and come pick up a magazine to beat the monotony of being in the hospital. But Phoenix VA leadership either didn't understand that or didn't care.

Although the relocation had been planned for a while, the move itself was a rush job. In their infinite wisdom, the powers that be scheduled it to take place over a weekend. We left a sunlit library on Friday and were unpacking books in the bowels of the building on Monday. I was, literally, at rock bottom, banished to the basement.

But I have to admit that while I shared the dismay of my library colleagues, I was beginning to feel better. Since Rep. Miller's April 9 hearing, it was becoming easier and easier to get up in the morning. I'd hop out of bed, grab the morning paper, and my spirits would be lifted as I saw story after story and editorial after editorial that further exposed the scandal. Bill and I joked, calling the papers and stories "pennies from heaven." I saved almost all of them.

When Sharon, Lance, and Brad Curry were put on administrative leave, I could not help but recall my premonition a year or so earlier of Lance and Sharon being escorted off the hospital campus. Sure, I only saw two of them in my vision, but two out of three isn't bad. That said, three out of three is even better.

33
A Changing of the Guard

Somewhere between the headlines and "resignations," I got a call from David Trudeau, the Office of Special Counsel lawyer who had been assigned to my whistleblower reprisal case. He asked if I'd heard from the Phoenix VA regional counsel about a settlement. I told him I hadn't. He said he had called their lawyers a few times asking them to speed things up, especially given what was happening with Lance and Sharon. I told David we had never heard a word from them. He said they'd be reaching out to me; you could say I was skeptical. Making me wait was just more of the VA standard operating procedure – delay, deflect, ignore.

Around this time, Stephanie Renslow's parents were having some health issues, so she had to pull back a bit from my representation. Even so, she continued to reach out to the VA. Their dialogue back and forth was disgusting and insulting. Department lawyers dismissed her, saying she wasn't really a "lawyer." They questioned the legitimacy of her role as my representative. They ran her around in circles and engaged her in a war of email and letter writing with the regional counsel. Each letter, each email, and each phone call was costing me money, and our already out-of-control expenses were continuing to add up, ballooning to more than $75,000. But, again, this was how VA worked. It buries you in paperwork, drowns you in expenses, and does whatever it takes to run the clock out to get you to quit.

As we were assembling a new legal team, Roger referred me to a noted federal case law attorney in Arlington, Va. named Peter Broida. We set up a phone call, and he confirmed everything Roger had said all along. The charges were bogus. VA was reaching. The department wanted to punish me through firing or demotion. And I had to fight back. It was true, all of it. Even so, it could not hide the reality that about eighteen months into the "30-day investigation," VA was digging in its heels and showing no sign of compromise, and Bill and I and our family were paying the price which, I'm sure, was part of their strategy.

Peter was writing a law book at the time and couldn't take my case. He directed me to a firm in Denver, Minahan & Muther, which represented federal employees and unions in termination and disciplinary actions. We contacted the firm and were put in touch with one of the attorneys, Josh Klinger, who would later become a name partner. After a brief conversation – and after researching his credentials – I knew he was the right fit. Roger and I hoped so, anyway. It was our third change in representation. With any luck, the third time would be a charm.

In addition to being well-versed in Equal Employment Opportunity law, the Office of Special Counsel, and Merit System Protection Board law, Josh knew that in cases like mine, the best battle plan was to bide your time and acknowledge the fact that this was a waiting game. So, here I was on the one hand trying to wait it out, and on the other hand trying to fight it out. I was frustrated, to say the least. How do you win by standing still against an institution that is coming at you from every direction? I tried to explain that to Josh, showing him the stacks of letters I'd already written and drafts of those I wanted to send. I explained that Roger and Stephanie reviewed and edited each one, and then decided which to send. (Sometimes Stephanie would pull the zingers out of mine - and insert them in hers.)

Josh read the first few letters I had crafted for him. He thought they were valid and contained a lot of good points. Then he said, "Stop the letter writing." I was dismayed, and kind of confused. If what I was saying had legitimacy, why not send them? "Because" he replied, "in this game, whoever speaks first loses. They want to know what you're doing, and every letter you send gives them more insight into your efforts and the misery they are inflicting upon you." I didn't like hearing that. I'd been treading water too damned long. Josh said it was my call, but he advised me to discontinue the letter writing. Reluctantly, I agreed.

Josh believed that we were rapidly reaching the point where VA had to move on my case. Sharon and Lance had been put on leave. I'd been banished to the basement. VA wasn't responding to the Office of Special Counsel. The bad headlines kept stacking up. The department was starting to hemorrhage, and its Band Aid approach was showing signs of collapse. Josh thought time was on my side and that something would give way and break in my direction. I just needed to stay strong and let things play out. Something would happen.

Then one day, something did. Out of the blue, I got an unexpected phone call. My personal story of whistleblower retaliation, which had largely been local and constrained by Lance's gag order, was about to go national.

34
SLIGHTLY KAFKAESQUE

David Fahrenthold joined the *Washington Post* in 2000, and his beats included Congress and the federal government. He'd later go on to win the Pulitzer Prize for National Reporting in 2017 for his coverage of Donald Trump and the president's claims of giving millions of dollars to charity. He's been a contributor to CNN, NBC News, and MSNBC. But in the summer of 2014, before the presidential campaign madness was in full bloom, he was interested in something else: whistleblower retaliation in the U.S. government. That led him to me.

It was twenty months into my exile. I had regularly been speaking with Eric Hannel and the Office of Special Counsel, both of whom had been pleading with the VA to do something about my case. We got nowhere – no movement, no big surprise. I was still feeling somewhat frustrated by playing Josh's waiting game, even though I fully understood his rationale and believed he was right. But as I've said, it's hard for me to not do something,

185

to sit back and let the world manage me. I'm not wired that way. So, when David called, I saw it as an opportunity.

I discussed his interview request with the OSC, and they didn't say yes or no. They did, however, say that sometimes, in cases like this, a news story could help someone's case. In dealing with the OSC, I asked David Trudeau if I could get in touch with the office's PR person. This led me to Nick Schwellenbach. When we first met over the phone, Nick told me about his job, why he supported OSC, and much of what he had learned about whistleblower retaliation. When we spoke about my case, he took an interest and offered to go talk to David, to learn more about what was going on with me. The nice thing about being in touch with Nick was that it gave me some public relations insight to focus on. But I digress.

After another round of discussions with Roger and Josh, and looping Nick in to talk about the media request from David Fahrenthold, we all agreed that OSC was right and that talking to the *Post* was a chance for me to get my story onto the national scene. Not only that, but given the *Post* is D.C.'s paper of record, the story would very likely end up on the desk of everyone at VA who had been systematically ignoring my situation.

For my own protection, we had to set ground rules for the interview. I was still fearful of Lance's gag order. Even though he had been put on leave, he still had his acolytes in the hospital, and I had no doubt they could (and would) still do his bidding. Beyond that, VA still had said and done nothing about a prospective settlement despite nudging from the OSC and others. Maybe something was in the works, maybe not. But we couldn't risk taking a wrong step that might gum up the works – or get me fired.

With all that in mind, we decided that the interview had to be done after hours or on the weekend because, as a private citizen, what I did on my own time was my business and no one else's.

186

David came to our house on the weekend for the interview. He said he was trying to understand one thing: Why was the government operating in this way? I would be an on-the-record source, as would a man named Walter Tamosaitas, a federal contractor with the Energy Department who faced retaliation after he raised red flags about the processing of radioactive waste.

David asked a lot of searching questions, not only about what had happened, but also how it affected me personally and professionally. In some ways, it was a healing process, talking so openly about everything. I also think it was the first time I saw myself as a true whistleblower. I saw something else, too. David had arranged for a freelance photographer, Samantha Sais, to come in and take pictures. When she showed them to me, I was knocked back. I looked so worn and tired. The dark cloud of trauma seemed to have blocked out my naturally sunny disposition. It was disconcerting, to say the least.

After Samantha left and we'd finished the interview, David asked, "What if I came to the library to see you at work tomorrow?" The request gave me pause. I was walking a fine line between Lance's gag order and possibly skirting the medical center guidelines by encouraging press access to the VA grounds unescorted, and David had made a formal request to talk with me at the hospital and been turned down. But the pause was only for a few seconds.

"The library is open to the public," I told him. "If, as a member of the public, you want to visit, you have every right to visit. But if you do, I can't talk to you because that would violate VA policy." And probably cost me my job, I thought but didn't say.

David was fine with that, and then started peppering me with questions about how the library worked – the processes visitors had to go through, signing in, showing ID, that sort of thing. I shared the procedures for using the computers, checking out books, or just coming in and reading the magazines and newspapers that were on the racks. As far as the world knew, he would be John Q. Public.

That's just how he appeared when he walked in the next morning around nine. I hadn't told anyone who he was or why he would show up in the basement library of the Phoenix VA, and when he arrived, he could have been anybody. He glanced around the space, found the rack of magazines and newspapers, and picked up a few for his "reading pleasure." Obviously, I didn't interact with him. I just kept right on doing my work. But I knew I was being watched, and I knew David was listening. That's what great reporters do: They observe. For a change, I wasn't being watched by vengeful supervisors who wanted my head on a platter but by someone who genuinely wanted to know what it was like to be a whistleblower facing reprisal. I have to say, after all those months of looking over my shoulder at every turn, it felt good.

Around 11:30, I left my station. David and I had agreed the night before that we'd meet for lunch (my personal time) before he went to California to gather materials for another story he was working on about Medicare fraud. When he picked me up in his rental car outside the hospital, I was thrilled. I realize that in all my years as a public affairs officer, I'd been in the presence of a lot of reporters. This was different, though. I mean, this was a reporter from the *Washington Post*, doing a story that involved me. I tried to be cool and to contain my excitement. I'm not entirely sure I was successful.

Over lunch, he asked more questions about my daily routine. I described the sheer drudgery of it all, especially compared to my service as a public relations specialist. He also said he'd like additional material for his story, including logs of my activities in the library so he could see exactly what I was working on (or not) while I was banished to the basement. What I sent him was hardly scintillating, showing that my jobs included getting the daily newspaper from the hospital canteen, putting away and checking out books, stocking paper in the printer, and prepping the fax machine. At least one task was worthwhile: helping veterans with the library's computers. Many are indigent and can't afford their own computers, so they use the ones available at public institutions like the VA. It's a small thing, I know, but it mattered to them – and to me.

After David returned to Washington from California, he would call me to verify the accuracy of his story. A day or two before it was set for publication, he said he needed to close the loop with Jean Simpson, the public affairs officer with the Veterans Integrated Service Network, who had denied his original request to talk with me at the hospital. She and I had worked together for years, and while she was supportive when all of this started to happen, she later stepped away from me. As I've said, a lot of people did. Fear of persecution from your supervisors can be a strong motivator. Later, she told me, "Paula, it was hard to defend the indefensible of what they did to you." Nice sentiment, I guess.

Anyway, David sent her an email saying the story was coming out. VA was officially on notice.

On Aug. 3, 2014, the story hit. It was on Page 1 of the *Washington Post*, headlined, "For whistleblowers, a bold move can be followed by one to department basement." The lead paragraphs read:

> PHOENIX — On her 71st workday in the basement, Paula Pedene had something fun to look forward to. She had an errand to run, up on the first floor.

189

"Today, I get to go get the papers. Exciting!" she said. "I get to go upstairs and, you know, see people."

The task itself was no thrill: Retrieve the morning's newspapers and bring them back to the library of the Phoenix Veterans Affairs hospital. The pleasure was in the journey. Down a long, sunlit hallway. Back again, seeing friends in the bustle of the hospital's main floor.

Then, Pedene got back in the elevator and hit "B." The day's big excitement was over. It was 7:40 a.m.

"I will not be able to do this forever," Pedene said later that day.

He went on to write that when he tried to get VA to explain what had happened to me, things got "slightly Kafkaesque." Jean Simpson said that she couldn't answer the question, deftly dodging by explaining, "Why she was moved to the library was Ms. Helman's decision." When David asked if Sharon could explain it, Jean said no. Noting that Sharon had been put on leave, he wrote, "So the person who forced Pedene out of her office has been forced out of *her* office. Has anybody checked to see whether Pedene should get out of the basement now?" Jean said she couldn't answer that either. "Since these are personnel actions, we are unable to provide any comment," she told him.

David's tone in the story was balanced, and if he felt any outrage at the injustices to me and other whistleblowers, it didn't creep through. (There's a reason he won the Pulitzer.) But as I read between the lines, I could almost feel in his words that he was shaking his head at how quickly and harshly the federal government could turn on one of its own for simply telling the truth. He didn't play the blame game either, but he had a telling quote from Tom Devine, a member of the watchdog group

Government Accountability Project: "There's a long, rich tradition of exiling whistleblowers to dusty, dark closets, or hallways, or public spaces."

Banishment was a tradition. Retaliation was the norm.

David closed his story (which also had a picture of me on the jump page), with this:

> Back in the basement of the Phoenix hospital, Pedene's day unspooled slowly. Somebody asked her how to repair his home printer. Someone needed help printing a résumé. Somebody needed her to look up Home Depot in the phone book.
>
> "What can you do?" a woman in a doctor's coat asked Pedene, inquiring quietly about her situation.
>
> "Nothing," Pedene told her. "Just hope it gets better."
>
> This was a rare good moment: a friend who'd ventured downstairs into the hospital basement. But eventually, the friend revealed why she was there.
>
> "But anyway," she said, "I'm looking for a copy machine."

I believe the story was a turning point.

What was happening to me was not a secret to anyone at the hospital, but the leadership was less than happy with the article, to put it mildly. Sharon was on leave, so Susan Bowers, the VISN director, was left to deal with the aftermath, and the reaction internally was pretty strong. I'd done everything by the books, though no one knew the degree to which I'd worked with David. It was a mess of their own making and, not to make a judgment (or much of one), there was nobody at the hospital who had an inkling of how to deal with a media crisis.

191

If Phoenix VA was unhappy, the VA in Washington was mortified. Bob McDonald had just been confirmed as the Secretary of Veterans Affairs, replacing Sloan Gibson, who had been serving as acting secretary since Gen. Shinseki resigned. After Rep. Miller's April hearing, D.C., like the rest of the world, knew about the scheduling scandal. What or how much they knew about leadership's attacks on me is an open question. Delay, deflect, and deceive had worked as a strategy for months, and over time, maybe the powers on high just thought they could either wait it out or sweep it under the rug.

But when David's story broke, there was no hiding or sweeping. I think VA also realized it could not ride this one out. Secretary McDonald and Sloan Gibson didn't want my issue in their laps. They knew something had to be done, and fast. I started to feel like the end was truly in sight.

35

VINDICATION (SORT OF)

O n Aug. 26, 2014, Sam and I – as well as the other truth-tellers at the hospital – were vindicated. More or less.

The VA's Office of Inspector General released its final report on the Wait Time Scandal. It reviewed VA and non-VA medical records of patients who died waiting for care, as well as more than one million email messages, 190,000 files from eleven encrypted computers or other devices, and 800,000 messages from "Veterans Heath Information Systems and Technology Architecture." Written by Inspector General Robert Griffin, the findings included:

- "Access barriers adversely affected the quality of primary and specialty care."
- "They (*patients*) frequently encountered obstacles when they or their providers attempted to establish care, when they needed outpatient appointments after hospitalizations or ED (*Emergency Department*) visits, and when seeking care while traveling or temporarily living in Phoenix."

193

- "We were able to identify 40 patients who died while on the EWL (*electronic wait list*) during the period April 2013 through April 2014."

- "Eleven staff stated they 'fixed' or were instructed to 'fix' appointments with wait times greater than 14 days. They did this by rescheduling the appointment for the same date and time but with a later desired date."

- "Twenty-eight staff stated they either printed out or received printouts of patient information for scheduling purposes. Staff said they kept the printouts in their desks for days or sometimes weeks before the veterans were scheduled an appointment or placed on the EWL. PVAHCS (*Phoenix*) executives and senior clinical staff were aware that their subordinate staff were using inappropriate scheduling practices."

- "The emphasis by Ms. Sharon Helman, the Director of PVAHCS, on her 'Wildly Important Goal' (WIG) effort to improve access to primary care resulted in a misleading portrayal of veterans' access to patient care. Despite her claimed improvements in access measures during fiscal year (FY) 2013, we found her accomplishments related to primary care wait times and the third-next available appointment were inaccurate or unsupported."

- "(T)he breakdown of the ethics system within VHA (*Veterans Health Administration*) contributed significantly to the questioning of the reliability of VHA's reported wait time data. VHA's audit, directed by the former VA Secretary in May 2014 following numerous allegations, also found that inappropriate scheduling practices were a systemic problem nationwide."

- "(W)ait time manipulations were prevalent throughout VHA."
- "PVAHCS maintained what we determined to be unofficial wait lists, and used inappropriate scheduling processes, which delayed veterans' access to health care services."

The report was 143 pages long and contained a laundry list of other findings: 3,500 veterans who were not on the electronic wait lists (EWL) but on "unofficial" lists; 1,800 veterans who wanted primary care appointments but were not on the EWL; a July 2, 2012 email from Sharon to Dr. Deering admitting there were delays in access to care of up to "a year long in some clinics"; an email from Dr. Christopher Burke, chief of primary care services, to Dr. Deering, dated Feb. 4, 2014 that said, "The fact that we currently have an EWL (with 1000+ pts on it) suggests that we cannot get a new patient appointment within 90 days. So how can we get a new patient appointment within 14 days? And how can we do it at a 50% rate? Or 40%? Or 30, or 20, or even 10%? It makes no sense."

The insanity of it all may have been best captured in an email from another facility in the VA system to Dr. Burke, asking how Phoenix was able to get new patient wait times down to seven days from 238 days. His reply: "Can I just say smoke and mirrors?"

Pretty cut and dried, right? Everything we had been saying – and everything leadership had been denying – was right there in black and white. So why did I say we were all "more or less" vindicated? In the executive summary of the report, Robert Griffin wrote that "we are unable to conclusively assert that the absence of timely quality care caused the deaths of these veterans." Interestingly, the language was virtually identical to what was in an Aug. 18, 2014 memo from Bob McDonald to the acting inspector general in which the VA secretary wrote, "OIG was unable to conclusively assert that the absence of timely care caused the death of these Veterans."

Unbelievable.

On the one hand, OIG laid out charge after charge, backed by evidence and documents and interviews that proved beyond any reasonable doubt veterans died waiting for care. On the other, Mr. Griffin still toed the department line that while tragic things happened, none of it was related to the simple fact that veterans faced months-long delays to see a doctor.

The response from the non-VA physician community was pretty skeptical. As Dennis Wagner wrote in the *Republic*, health-care experts "say Griffin's report used a measure that is not consistent with pathology practices because no matter how long a patient waits for care, the underlying 'cause' of death will be a medical condition rather than the delay." He continued: "Put simply, people die of pneumonia, heart conditions and bullet wounds — not waiting to see the doctor." He went on to quote a chief medical examiner in Jefferson County, Alabama, who said, "I can't imagine a circumstance where someone would word it that way."

In a Veterans Affairs committee hearing on Sept. 9, 2014, Nevada Sen. Dean Heller was highly critical of Mr. Griffin's language and the OIG's conclusion. "I don't want to give the VA a pass on this, and that's exactly what this line does," Heller told Dr. John Daigh, assistant inspector general for health-care inspections, referring to the "unable to conclusively assert" verbiage. "It exonerates the VA of any responsibility in past manipulation of these wait times." All of which was well and good, and appreciated by those of us who had been fighting the lies, but it did not erase the headlines that accompanied the OIG's final report, such as, "Overblown claims of death and waiting times at the VA" (*Washington Post*) and "IG: Shoddy care by VA didn't cause Phoenix death" (*Associated Press*). As Dennis wrote, "many media outlets cast the investigative report as vindication for the VA and as refutation of Arizona whistle-blower claims."

VA was doing what it does best – spinning. That's their response to veterans who had died tragically because of the ambitions, hunger for power, and above-it-all mentality of the leadership in Phoenix. It seemed as if ignoring the facts, twisting the story, creating a new narrative, all shared a single goal: to provide cover for their own. That's what bureaucracies sometimes do; they shield the protected class they created, in this case, the leadership at the Phoenix VA. From what we saw, the VA bureaucrats were able to survive and get promoted or moved to another position to save them, while the veterans died. And nobody in a position to make a clear judgment about that seemed to get it. That's not what I signed up for. It's not what any of us signed up for.

36
How to Lie with Statistics

Sometime between the Aug. 24 OIG report and a Sept. 17 House Veterans Affairs Committee hearing, a series of books came into the library for a newly minted supervisor training course that Sharon, Lance, and Dr. Deering had requested. As I was helping to catalogue them and set them aside for leadership, one caught my eye. It was titled *How to Lie with Statistics*, written by Darrell Huff, who included this in the introduction: "This book is a sort of primer in ways to use statistics to deceive. It may seem altogether too much like a manual for swindlers." Technically, the author wrote it to educate the uninformed on how to spot and question statistics that are shady or outright false. But it was also a primer on how manipulators manipulate data for their own ends, and the many ways it could be done.

Sound familiar?

I asked my supervisor, Mark Simmons, if I could check it out for review, and he agreed. Then I looked at the sixteen supervisors who were slated for training and saw that the list included several of Sharon's (how can I put this diplomatically?) brown noses. That night, thumbing through the book at home, I could not help but be struck by a chapter called "How to Statisculate," which Mr. Huff said was a made-up word that meant statistical manipulation. He noted that "the distortion of statistical data and its manipulation to an end are not always the work of professional statisticians."

"What comes full of virtue from the statistician's desk," he continued, "may find itself twisted, exaggerated, oversimplified, and distorted-through-selection by a salesman, a public relations expert, a journalist, or an advertising copywriter."

Or, to put it in the context of my current realm, the VA leadership in Phoenix.

I couldn't believe what I was reading. After everything that had happened at the hospital – a lot of it based around data that had been perverted to hide or distort the facts – here was a how-to book offering what amounted to advice on ways to manipulate. I was equal parts concerned, outraged, and incredulous. I quickly got on the phone to Eric Hannel and told him about the book and how it was part of a new heath care leadership class VA was deploying. He thanked me and said he'd get his hands on a copy.

He did, and then he got it in the hands of Rep. Tim Huelskamp, a member of the House Veterans Affairs Committee who had earned a bachelor's degree in social science education and a doctorate in political science and was formerly a statistical analyst. Put those three areas of expertise together – social science, politics, and statistics – and throw them on top of a book about how to manipulate data, and you're probably going to start a fire. Which is exactly what happened.

Rep. Huelskamp held the hearing on Sept. 17 about long wait times and other issues in Phoenix. The witnesses included Dr. Lisa Thomas, Chief of Staff of the Veterans Health Administration, and Dr. Darren Deering, the Phoenix VA hospital's Chief of Staff.

In the library, I told staff I needed to watch this hearing, and as it was around lunchtime, they were able to cover for me. I put my headphones on, focusing on the computer monitor while the witnesses were questioned about allegations regarding whistleblower retaliation and data manipulation. Then it happened. Rep. Huelskamp held up the book. He grilled Dr. Deering about its use, focusing specifically on a graph/chart hospital leadership had provided that purportedly compared the rise in outpatient visits with the number of fulltime employees at the Phoenix VA. As the *Republic* reported:

"At a glance, the graph appears to show that growth in outpatient visits far exceeded the increase in number of employees from fiscal 2010 to 2014. But a closer look shows the two measures in the graph were created on far different scales, inaccurately comparing the growth in outpatient visits with the growth in employees."

The manipulation of that data, the congressman said, was basically straight out of the book.

I remember looking over at another library tech, Ray Small (who was more on Sharon's side than on mine). We locked eyes for a second, then I went back to watching. In a moment, I heard Ray call out to Mark Simmons, telling him to come to the computer and look at what was going on. He did, seeing the book on camera, then Mark immediately glanced at me. I could see the fear in his eyes. He knew there would probably be repercussions.

As for me, it felt a little like I had turned the last corner. I wasn't afraid anymore. When the Sept. 17 hearing ended, I went straight into Mark's office and told him exactly what I had done. He asked me if I still had the book checked out and in my possession. I told him I did, and that I'd called Eric, and that the committee had secured it on its own. As it turned out, the book had already been used to train about 500 VA employees at other medical centers.

When Secretary Bob McDonald saw and heard about the book during the hearing, he was understandably mad. He was a compassionate leader and was sensitive to the department's credibility and image, but he also understood the implications of using this particular book in supervisor training – to say nothing of the deceitful practices it described. The wreckage he'd been appointed to clean up just kept getting worse. He ordered that the book no longer be used, sending an email to VA employees that read in part, "I have not read and am not commenting on the merits of the book.

"Let me be clear — anything that is contrary to our mission of serving veterans, in perception or practice, or which does not align with our I-CARE core values — Integrity, Commitment, Advocacy, Respect, and Excellence — will not be tolerated in the open and accountable culture we want in this new VA."

We pulled the book off the shelves the next day. Neither Mark nor I faced any repercussions. Sometimes you have to choose your fights. This was one the VA simply could not win.

In addition to erasing my fear, the book episode at the hearing had another impact on me. It was looking like the curtain was beginning to fall, as if this was my final act of endurance. I felt like the angels were telling me, "You've done your work. It's time to move on." Oddly enough, I think the VA leadership – not really known for paying any attention to their or anyone else's better angels – may have finally been hearing the same thing.

37
SETTLEMENT

My angels were right.

One afternoon shortly thereafter, I got a call from Eric Bachman, deputy director of the Office of Special Counsel, whom I had met previously when he came to Phoenix for a meeting. We had discussed my case at the time, but all he could tell me was the OSC was trying to break it free of an ongoing FBI review. Even though he was not certain when that would happen, he assured me it probably would...eventually. That made sense. Despite Lance's best efforts, VA had been unable to find anything criminal or negligent against me, including Bill's access to the VA computer to upload photos. However, they now had a ton of information and evidence we had provided that proved the existence of the secret wait lists, the cover-ups that occurred when the paper lists were hidden or destroyed when audits like the Joint Commission came to Phoenix, the staff departures caused by a hostile work environment, whistleblower retaliation, and so much more. So, while I was still playing the waiting game by someone else's rules, there was at least reason for a glimmer of optimism.

Eric said that he and Adam Miles, the Deputy Special Counsel for policy and congressional affairs at OSC, had been working with VA on some whistleblower cases, and mine was among the first they were reviewing. He asked if I wanted to continue pursuing the case through the Phoenix VA Regional Counsel or bump it up to the VA Office of General Counsel. Um, let's see. The Phoenix VA regional counsel had done everything in its power to delay action and cover up the evidence I had reported. It had also consistently supported Sharon and Lance, and left me hanging, which violated policy and procedure. It had also done nothing to advance a settlement as requested by OSC in April. I thought about it for, I don't know, a nanosecond. We moved my case to the Office of General Counsel.

From that point on, negotiations went into full swing. A big focus of the discussions revolved around what job I would have. All I really wanted was what I'd wanted all along – to return to my previous position as public affairs officer in Phoenix. Both Eric and Adam understood but cautioned against it. They said there were still people at the hospital who were not happy about what I'd done (that would be Lance and Sharon's "yes" people, many of whom were still comfortably in place), and that they were in a position to make my life miserable. I pushed back at first. I loved my job, and I'd missed doing it. It had been wrongfully stolen from me, and I was not in the least interested in letting that indignity stand. But the more we talked, the more I realized Eric and Adam were right. My critics were never going to forgive or forget, and there was little doubt they'd look for even the smallest ways to get even. I let it go, leaving my favorite job while agreeing to take a position as a senior communications specialist for the Office of Communications at the Veterans Health Administration.

With that large sticking point behind us (I had tried for months to get my position back as the public affairs officer in Phoenix), my settlement – the details of which, financial and otherwise, are confidential – fell into place. I have to say that with all the highs (exposing the scandal) and lows (Sharon, Lance, and their shenanigans) of the previous twenty-two months, there was still a voice deep inside my head that kept saying, this isn't over until it's over. Then OSC called and asked for my permission to send out a news release announcing the settlement agreements with me. That made it official. I could now wake up from the nightmare.

The release was dated Sept. 29, 2014 and also focused on Kate Mitchell and Damian Reese, who had also endured retaliation from administrators – something Sam and I knew all too well. Kate had been transferred out of her job as an Emergency Department physician after filing complaints with leadership about deteriorating conditions in the ED. She'd highlighted when and how leadership was risking patients' lives. Damian had raised alarms inside the hospital with his ethics consult, raising concerns over falsified wait time data, and wrote the email saying that the practices were "unethical and a disservice to our veterans" (and ultimately got K.J. Sloan removed from her role as Ethics Officer). He had given me the ethics consult that Sharon buried, which I passed along to Sam to share with CNN because I knew it would help underscore the argument that, yep, we warned them and others about the lack of care for our nation's veterans. He was able to claim whistleblower status after leadership marked down his performance review based upon his complaint about their "lack of ethics in sharing the truth." After the letter aired on CNN, Damian had an inkling I was the one who gave the letter to Sam, who then gave it to CNN, but Damian never confronted me about it. I felt bad about not telling him. Then one day, after Sharon was put on leave, I summoned up the nerve to tell him and apologized. "I'm not mad, Paula," he said. "I'm glad. It had to be done."

In the news release, I said, "I feel vindicated and happy and sad. There are so many mixed emotions. I'm moving forward and looking forward." It also noted that I had been "banished to work in a basement library," that the actions taken against me included "a challenge of (my) disability as well as allegations that resulted in criminal and administrative investigations," and that I had worked "behind the scenes" with Sam Foote to bring the Wait Time Scandal to light.

It also included this quote from me:

"My hope is that settlements like these will help change the VA culture. What remains to be seen is how far it will go. I think the way to answer that is to have accountability and disciplinary action against those who reprised against me."

But whether that eventually happened – accountability and disciplinary action – and whether the VA culture changed would both be up for debate in the aftermath that followed.

38
AFTERMATH

I transferred to my new job on Oct. 4, 2014, becoming a "virtual" employee based in Phoenix but assigned to Washington, D.C. The arrangement seemed better for me. As one who is legally blind and can't drive, I was continuously having to find carpools, buses, vanpools, and other ways to get to work at the Phoenix VA. After twenty years of scrambling for transportation, I guess it was time to at least let that stress go. However, I also knew that in just sitting at home, I'd miss the patients, the staff, and the community members that had been such an important part of life. Still, the experience of the past nearly two years was raw in my heart and mind. By going virtual, I could take some time to heal.

Based on the whistleblower evidence I had provided to the Office of Special Counsel and others, I was called to testify in the removal of Sharon Helman and later Lance Robinson. I provided the information under oath to Mike Culpepper and Joe Davis from the Office of Accountability Review. I supplied them with dozens of documents and gave them contact information of people who could corroborate what I had shared. All were verified. All showed the truth. And it paid off.

On June 20, I received a letter from John Young, an attorney with the disclosure unit of the Office of Special Counsel. It stated, "We have concluded that there is a substantial likelihood that the information you provided discloses a violation of law, rule, or regulation, gross mismanagement, an abuse of authority, and specific danger to public health and safety. Accordingly, we are referring this information to the Secretary of Veterans Affairs for an investigation and report."

Five months later, On Nov. 24, 2014, Sharon was "formally removed" from her position in Phoenix after being on paid administrative leave for six months. In a statement, VA said, "This removal action underscores VA's commitment to hold leaders accountable and ensure that Veterans have access to quality and timely care." A year later, VA said she could keep her bonus of $9,080 for meeting performance goals in 2013. On May 16, 2016, she was sentenced to two years' probation – not for her role in the scandal, but for accepting about $50,000 in gifts from a "friend" who was a lobbyist and failing to disclose them. The gifts included an $11,000 visit to Disneyland, a car, a $5,000 check, spa visits, and tickets to a Beyoncé concert.

The "friend" was Max Lewis, a onetime VA executive who had been Sharon's boss and mentor before he became a lobbyist for a company that received millions in VA contracts. In the sentencing hearing, Sharon cried. "Serving veterans was truly my life's passion, and I am proud of my work," she said. (No comment.) "I should have disclosed the gifts I received from a personal friend, but I did not. That was a betrayal." She also said she had given her "heart and soul to caring for veterans." (No further comment.) The friend was subsequently fired from his job for violating the firm's "long-standing ethics policy." (For what it's worth, newspaper reports revealed that Lewis had set up addresses in the cities where Sharon worked, including Spokane, a Chicago suburb, and Phoenix. Make of that what you will.)

Sharon sued to get her job back, arguing that some parts of a reform law passed in 2014 in the wake of the scandal – the Veterans Access, Choice, and Accountability Act – were unconstitutional and denied her an avenue to appeal. Then-Attorney General Loretta Lynch sided with her legal arguments and said the Justice Department would not defend the reform. Critics responded by saying that Lynch's decision basically paved the way for Sharon to return to her position.

On May 9, 2017, a federal appeals court overturned her firing, which had previously been upheld by an administrative judge. While the intent of the 2014 law was to speed the removal of VA executives for gross misconduct, the court ruled that Sharon should have had a chance to appeal the judge's decision to the U.S. Merit Systems Protection Board. The expedited removal and appeals authority that was granted under the law was unconstitutional, the appeals court said. But as of this writing, she is still fired, likely because of the felony charges for accepting the "gifts" (bribes?) for steering business to Max (who had followed her cross-country) and his consulting firm.

Lance went back to work at the hospital for a short time in 2016 after being on paid leave for almost two years. But VA finally filed charges against him for negligent performance of duties and failing to provide accurate information, among other allegations. I had to testify against him at the Sandra Day O'Connor building in Phoenix. I was not intimidated, anxious, or rattled. The VA lawyers came to prep me, and it was clear they had a strong case. And while I'm not really an eye-for-an-eye person, I'd be lying if I said I felt no satisfaction in turning the tables on him. He was fired on June 8, and the Merit System Protection Board upheld the decision. Lance appealed, telling the court that he did not know the scheduling records were false and saying he could not be blamed for the "failings of subordinates." In August 2019, the U.S. Court of Appeals in Washington, D.C. determined the firing was proper, ruling in part:

"The question here is whether Mr. Robinson was negligent in that he knew or should have known that his subordinates consistently failed to use scheduling practices required by VA policy. In short, the answer is yes…(H)e took a hands-off approach to managing the scheduling problems at Phoenix VA despite knowing the severity of scheduling problems permeating the system."

This wasn't news, at least to Sam and me. We had been sending off anonymous letters to investigatory bodies, and we knew they were being shared with Phoenix VA leaders, but they'd just circle the wagons. We would disclose allegations through official channels (like VA leadership), but rather than those allegations being investigated by the Office of Inspector General, they would be passed on to the very leaders we'd called into question. Then, since self-preservation is their Job One, they'd cover everything up. We could never really disclose everything through traditional channels, and instead saved the "hammers" for outside bodies like House Veterans Affairs Committee or the Office of Special Counsel. So, when the appeals court said Lance "knew or should have known" about what was going on in Phoenix, there's not a shred of doubt in my mind that he absolutely knew. Sharon may have ruled the quagmire, but he was her enforcer.

They weren't the only ones who lost their jobs. Brad Curry and Dr. Darren Deering were both fired on June 8, 2016 as well, for what the VA called "negligent performance of duties and failure to provide effective oversight for not ensuring Veterans were either properly scheduled for appointments or placed on an appropriate wait list." But in the end, the firings pretty much stopped there, and VA even played the statistics game when talking about dismissals to that point.

In February 2015, Secretary McDonald said in a television interview that VA had fired sixty people in the wait time scandal. Then the department had to scramble and say just fourteen had been fired and sixty others got lesser punishments. But a subsequent investigation by the *New York Times* found that eight of the agency's 280,000 employees had been punished for their involvement, and only one – Sharon – had been fired.

The beat, sadly, kept going on.

By May 2017, it was pretty clear – through court cases, firings, veterans' deaths, and settlements – that hospital executives in Phoenix had acted unethically at best, and borderline criminally. The evidence was overwhelming. Yet on May 4, the VA Office of Inspector General issued a report in response to "improprieties" that surfaced in the Wait Time Scandal. It was based on interviews with 190 employees and reviews of a million emails and thousands of documents. Now keep in mind that just three years earlier, OIG had issued a report that was pretty damning to Phoenix VA leadership. Contrast that with the conclusions of the May report:

"The joint VA OIG and FBI investigation found no evidence that there was any intentional, coordinated scheme by management to create a secret wait list, delay patient appointments, or manipulate wait time metrics. Specifically, regarding the EWL allegations, we found that implementation of the mandated EWL program was done very poorly at PVAHCS, resulting in many veterans experiencing extended wait times for Primary Care appointments. We found no evidence of any scheme initiated by VA management officials to willfully delay appointments or mischaracterize wait times. We found no secret lists used by anyone at the facility to hide patients waiting for care."

The fox was back guarding the henhouse, more than reinforcing Eric Hannel's description of the VA: It remains, even to this day, a self-licking ice cream cone.

39
SOMEONE HAD TO TAKE A STAND

In the wake of my settlement, and before all the post-scandal controversy heated up, I was preparing to give a speech about my experiences to the Rocky Mountain chapter of the Public Relations Society of America. As I have said, my professional colleagues with PRSA had stuck with me all along, and the announcement of my settlement broadened that support. What I didn't know at the time was that Jan Howard of the Tucson PRSA chapter, who I had served with when I was chair of the PRSA Western District, was compiling a case study about what I'd done. Her boyfriend was a veteran, and during my time as chair-elect and chair of the district they had come to know my experiences. She asked the Western District's board to nominate me for PR Pro of the Year. I'd never heard of the award and had no idea it even existed. As far as I was concerned, I had done what I thought was right, unaware of the journey – one of faith and perseverance – that would follow.

Anyway, while I was getting ready to make my remarks in Denver, Bill and I had just sat down to lunch. My phone rang, displaying an unknown number. Usually, I let those go to voice mail, but for some reason I picked up. It was Jim Roop, APR, Fellow PRSA, who told me that I had been selected as PR Pro of the Year. I was overcome with so much joy. As I was listening to Jim explain the merits of the award, I looked at Bill and started to cry. I couldn't believe it. When I hung up, I wept as I shared the news.

When the time came for my acceptance speech in November in Atlanta, I was nervous but also steadfast. I learned in my media prep with Sam that it was the story that mattered most, and to just tell it and speak straight from the heart. The night before, I listed the seven PRSA values on a single note card from the hotel. That was my "speech." When the time came, I walked backstage and then into the green room, cane in hand. I was elegantly escorted by Navy Capt. Brook DeWalt to accept the award. Brook got me to center stage and then stood back as I ambled over to the podium (trying to dial back my emotions, which wasn't easy). I glanced down at the note card and looked up at a sea of smiling faces from my fellow professionals, some of whom had had a front row seat to my ordeal. I was excited and deeply grateful.

After a lovely introduction from PRSA President and colleague Kathy Barbour, I began my remarks.

"I am so honored to be here as a U.S. Navy veteran and a PR practitioner, and I can tell you I am humbled to represent our profession, our military, and our veterans as I accept this honor.

"Many people may not know it, but today, as we are gathered here, there's one percent of our population who are watching our backs as they serve us with their military service in the Army, Navy, Marines, Air Force, Coast Guard, or Merchant Marines. To those military members who are with us today, can you please stand for a moment to be recognized?

"And in our country, they are followed by another group of people who have defended our freedoms. They are the seven percent of the population who have left military service and are now called our veterans. So, to any of our veterans who are out there today who served in the Army, Navy, Marines, Air Force, Coast Guard, or Merchant Marines, please stand for a moment so we may recognize you as well?

"To this eight percent, the other ninety-two percent say **thank you** for our freedoms. Your service allows us to assemble here today, to take part in this conference, to vote in our leadership venues, and much more. We owe you a debt of gratitude.

"As our society gathered together on Saturday for the Leadership Assembly, our CEO spoke about our seven PRSA Values. These include:

1. Respect for the Individual
2. Courage
3. Honesty/Integrity
4. A Servant's Heart
5. Innovation, Creativity and Risk Taking
6. A Commitment to Personal and Professional Growth, and
7. Achievement

"I want to take a moment to highlight a few that I know helped me during my twenty-two months of whistleblower reprisal when I was 'banished to the basement' by senior leaders at the Phoenix VA Health Care System. In my opinion, these leaders didn't share these values, as they believed it was okay to reprise against a service-disabled veteran.

"But what seemed to be okay for them wasn't okay for me or Dr. Sam Foote, who led the charge to expose the VA Wait Time Scandal. For folks like Sam, myself, and others, what they were doing needed to be stopped. Someone had to take a stand to fight it. Someone had to help our veterans, and that is what compelled Sam, myself, and others to collaborate and fight this battle against some pretty oppressing odds.

"So, of these PRSA values, which are the ones I felt were the most prominent in our lives during this time? Let's see if I can explain.…

"Did our fight take **courage**? One could say it did. Day after day, I had to go into the facility, where I once was the 'face of the VA', and work in a position seven notches below my pay grade. Here, I would help veterans, not with communications venues and media relations, but in checking out books, logging patients onto the library computers, faxing documents, providing support services such as making copies, and handing out pens and pencils. I did so with a smile, all the while living in a fog of depression. The depression came from knowing that there was so much good I could be doing in a communications realm for VA and yet, despite having the talent and ability to do so, I had to face the inability to do so while dealing with verified reprisal by senior leaders.

"Did it involve **honesty**? Yes, it did. According to the evidence, there was misleading information, and as a result, it was hindering the care to our nation's veterans. We knew that we would have to share our facts, convince people to listen to us and, in some cases, to take a stand for ethics even if it meant standing alone.

"Did it mean having **integrity**? Yes, it did. We were waging a battle with the most senior leaders at the Phoenix VA Health Care System. It was their word against ours, their word against the patients', and their word against those who were 'taken out of their jobs.' It was interesting to see how the battle unfolded. Among the staff there were those who were my steadfast supporters and who would constantly pray for me. There were those who began to question my ethics and integrity because, after all, I was "taken out of my job." And then there were those who willingly jumped on the reprisal bandwagon and constantly tried to throw us under the bus through their words, their efforts, and their abuse of leadership authority. For Sam, it was the senior leaders trying to paint a picture of him as a 'lazy doctor' to Congressional leaders. And to members of the media, to portray him as one who 'didn't know the numbers' or who didn't 'grasp the real effect of what they were doing.' Really? In our books, delayed care is denied care, and it needed to stop.

"Although it was stopped then, what still bothers me to this day is that some of those leaders are on paid administrative leave, while others are still in their jobs. To VA and our veterans, I think this is a disgrace. So, if you can join me in taking a stand, I hope you will by calling for #VAAccountability.

"Did our efforts take a **Servant's Heart?** We believe it did. We all know now that it was Dr. Foote who was telling the truth, and he paid a dear price for it. He had to retire from VA earlier than he had hoped. He had to throw rocks at an agency he adored. And he had to stand alone to expose the VA Wait Time Scandal. It was during this time that I helped Sam with public relations advice and counsel and to put him in touch with staff on the House Veterans Affairs Committee. To them and to Staffer Eric Hannel and Congressman Jeff Miller, who truly broke the story about the horror of the waits and delays in veterans' health care, we owe a debt of gratitude. We made it through by focusing on those who were supporting us – our families, our true friends, my legal team of Roger French, Josh Klinger, and others – and my wonderful PRSA colleagues nationally, in Phoenix, and through the Western District.

"Yet perhaps most importantly, it meant having faith in God. For you see, even though I didn't always handle the situation as well as I would have liked – I drank, I cried, and I lived in a gray fog for many months – in looking back at it now, I can honestly say that God had me where He needed me to be. And that is what matters the most.

"As a Phoenix VA Whistleblower, mine and my family's life will never be the same after being 'banished to the basement' or exposing the VA Wait Time Scandal, but what I can say is this, I'm ready for the future, whatever that may be, and I pray now to let God be THE guide in my life.

"I thank you for this honor, I'm truly humbled, I'm proud to be a member of PRSA, and I am truly proud to serve our veterans."

EPILOGUE

G iven the depth and reach of the VA Wait Time Scandal — it would eventually touch more than 110 hospitals in about twenty states — hopes for a quick fix were unreasonable. After eighteen inspector general reports, Congress had passed the $16.3 billion VA reform package in 2014 that included language boosting veterans' access to care and providing additional funds for doctors and nurses at VA hospitals. It wasn't the cure-all that veterans needed or deserved, but it was a start. After all, the problem didn't pop up overnight. It would not be solved overnight with a single piece of legislation. Still, the scandal dragged on, not only in Phoenix but also in places like Iowa City, Omaha, and Shreveport.

Meanwhile, VA Central Office in Washington seemed to be in a permanent state of disarray. The department had gone through all kinds of leadership changes at the top between 2014 and 2018. After Gen. Shinseki resigned, Bob McDonald was confirmed by a 97-0 vote in the Senate to become the new secretary. But despite widespread support for McDonald from veterans' groups, President Trump replaced him with David Shulkin, the Under Secretary of Veterans Affairs for Health. In 2018, the president fired Shulkin after an inspector general's finding that he improperly accepted gifts, misrepresented travel plans, used a VA employee as "a personal travel concierge," and lied about approvals of a 10-day trip to Denmark and London. (So much for ethics.)

Then the president named Robert Wilkie, formerly the Under Secretary for Personnel and Readiness in the Defense Department, as interim secretary, then announced plans to nominate his personal physician, Adm. Ronny L. Jackson, as Shulkin's permanent replacement. Shortly after that announcement, however, Dr. Jackson withdrew his name from consideration after reports surfaced questioning his professional conduct. The president then selected Mr. Wilkie who, in July 2018, was approved by the Senate on an 86-9 vote.

Despite all the chaos and the continuing trickle of stories that further exposed cracks in how the VA provided care to veterans, I was healing. For the most part, my depression had lifted. We were still working on helping Steven manage his mental health issues, and he was starting to thrive. Robert was back in school, working, and doing better than ever. Bill had earned his Master's degree and was happy again. Echoing the problems the department was dealing with in D.C., Phoenix was having a difficult time getting anyone to replace Sharon. The hospital went through five directors between 2014 and 2016. RimaAnn Nelson was appointed on Oct. 2, 2016 and stayed on through October 2019.

While Phoenix VA will always occupy a special (though sometimes painful) place in my heart, the hospital was mostly in my rear-view mirror. In 2018, four years after the scandal dam had broken, I was named acting director of the newly established VA

Office of Communications, Internal Communications. My job was to help rebuild employee confidence in a department and mission that had been battered for years by harsh headlines, negative reports, and critical congressional inquiries. I knew it would be a challenge, to say the least.

I was also appointed as the Communications Project Team Lead for Launching the VA MISSION Act, which was the newest piece of legislation passed by Congress to provide veterans with more choice in their health care options. This law is meant to stop delays. I am honored to say, our team won two national awards for launching the VA Mission Act, one for public service and the other for community outreach.

In these capacities, I was spending a lot of time in Washington D.C.. One day, when I walked into the front door of VA Central Office, I noticed a crowd of people at the foot of the stairs. When I asked what was going on, someone said Secretary Wilkie was at the top of the landing meeting employees. I veered towards the line of people and waited to meet him. As I made my way up, one of the secretary's aides asked my name, and I told her. It didn't register with her, but it did register with Jim Byrne, then the acting Deputy Secretary of VA, who was also on hand to screen staff before meeting the Secretary. But before he could put two and two together (I think he would have preferred to steer me away from the Secretary), there I was, talking with Secretary Wilkie. I introduced myself and shook his hand.

"Sir, I was one of the original whistleblowers in Phoenix," I told him.

He bent down to get a little closer to me. "You're what?"

"One of the Phoenix VA whistleblowers." There was a moment. Then I added, "I'm sorry about this mess. I hope it can be fixed."

"We have an old Sicilian saying in my family, Paula: There's nothing like truth to shame the devil."

"You're right. We had to do it. And it all worked out because God had me where He needed me to be. Faith sustained us."

"Yes," he replied. "Yes, it did."

I nodded and walked away.

Smiling.

Thank you for reading

A

SACRED

DUTY

How a Whistleblower took on the VA and won

We invite you to post a review on
Goodreads & your favorite online retailer.

For a free e-book, join our mailing list at:
www.SkyrocketPress.com

About the Authors

Paula Pedene is a decorated U.S. Navy Veteran with military service during both the Cold War and Operation Desert Storm. After transitioning from Navy Journalist, she became an award-winning Department of Veterans Affairs (VA) public relations practitioner. *A Sacred Duty* is Pedene's story of combining faith, perseverance, and grit to win her Whistleblower case, eventually leading to the resignation of the Secretary of Veterans Affairs. www.PaulaPedene.com

Doug Williams is a playwright, novelist, and award-winning screenwriter. His script based on the life of Texas Congresswoman Barbara Jordan has been recognized in over 25 film festivals, winning six best screenplay awards, and his plays have been produced in New York and regionally. Critics compared his most recent novel, the political thriller *Nowhere Man*, to *Homeland* and *House of Cards*. He is also a former journalist and served as a press secretary in the U.S. Senate.

ACKNOWLEDGMENTS

I did not set out to become a VA Whistleblower or a book author, yet both found me. As a 20-year dedicated and award-winning VA public relations specialist, I was at the top of my game in helping our nation's veterans at the Carl T. Hayden VA Medical Center. This hospital was a model of excellence.

Then our ship veered off course with several leadership changes until we found ourselves shipwrecked on a lawless island. The good people banded together with grit, and we found a way to send out an S-O-S. Once our message fell into the right hands, the rescue team came to our aid like knights riding white horses.

I give special thanks to my brothers and sisters, our dog Coco, the unbeatable Roger French, the strategic Dr. Sam Foote, the compassionate duo Rick and Carol Romley, the colorful Joe Abodeely, and the straightforward Josh Klinger. Thanks for the victory.

To House Veterans Affairs Oversight and Investigation Subcommittee Chairman Jeff Miller, his aide and Staff Director Eric Hannel, and Congressmember Ann Kirkpatrick, I owe a debt of gratitude for their efforts in saving the lives of veterans.

Media members also pitched in, including Investigative Reporter Dennis Wagner and editors of the *Arizona Republic*, Scott Pasmore, Drew Griffin, and Anderson Cooper from CNN.

Veterans from a nonprofit who knew we were telling the truth also jumped onboard, including Pete Hegseth, Dan Caldwell, and Darin Selnick from CVA.

After returning to solid ground, I shared the tale of my journey, only to be told I needed to put pen to paper so others could read it. I did as they suggested, and thanks to a fabulous colleague Doug Williams, who I met through a friend Bill Outlaw, the book transformed from a textbook journey to a compelling story.

Helping me refine and hone my book along the way was none other than M*A*S*H star Loretta Swit, whose love for veterans bound our friendship.

I also owe a debt of gratitude to the incredible team at the Fairmont Scottsdale Princess Spa, especially Jack Miller, Brennan Evans, and Valerie Lee, who gave me a place of refuge.

And to my loving family, my dear friends who stood by my side, my VA vanpool colleagues, my Public Relations Society of America members, and others, thanks for the lift you gave these wings.

To the hundreds of thousands of VA employees who ethically continue to care for our veterans or those who have borne the battle, we thank you and wish you God speed.

WEBSITE LINKS (CHRONOLOGICALLY)

VA official demoted after her testimony: *Arizona Republic*/AZ Central: http://archive.azcentral.com/news/arizona/articles/20130 314va-official-arizona-pedene-demoted-after-testimony.html?fullsite=true

Veterans Day Parade organizers say the Parade will go on, KJZZ Radio: https://kjzz.org/content/3566/veterans-day-Parade-organizers-say-Parade-will-go

After a year of upheaval, the Phoenix Veterans Day Parade is ready to rise again, *FrontDoors Media*: https://frontdoorsmedia.com/valley-veterans-day-Parade-2/

A fatal wait, veterans languish and die on a VA hospital's secret list, CNN: https://www.cnn.com/2014/04/23/health/veterans-dying-health-care-delays/index.html

CNN Special, VA hospital investigations: https://www.cnn.com/specials/us/va-hospitals

AZ Central Timeline, the road to the VA wait-time scandal:

https://www.azcentral.com/story/news/arizona/politics/20
14/05/10/timeline-road-va-wait-time-scandal/8932493/

Phoenix VA Officials Knew of False Data for Two Years,
Arizona Republic:
https://www.azcentral.com/story/news/arizona/investigati
ons/2014/06/22/phoenix-va-officials-false-
data/11232447/

Severe report finds VA hid waiting lists at hospitals, *NY
Times*: https://www.nytimes.com/2014/05/29/us/va-
report-confirms-improper-waiting-lists-at-phoenix-
center.html

Congressional Panel, Phoenix VA Wait Time Scandal,
CSPAN: https://www.c-span.org/video/?321497-
1/hearing-veterans-affairs-inspector-generals-report

Testimony places VA in greater disrepute, *Washington
Post*: https://www.washingtonpost.com/news/federal-
eye/wp/2014/07/08/testimony-places-va-in-greater-
disrepute/

Taking A Stand for Ethics, *Social Media Today*:
https://www.socialmediatoday.com/content/taking-stand-
ethics-and-accountability-pr-paula-pedene-apr

For whistleblowers, a bold move can be followed by one
to the department basement, *Washington Post*:
https://www.washingtonpost.com/politics/for-
whistleblowers-bold-move-can-be-followed-by-one-to-
department-basement/2014/08/03/39d12656-182f-11e4-
9e3b-
7f2f110c6265_story.html?noredirect=on&utm_term=.4c7
41ed16a2e

Phoenix VA whistleblowers receive retaliation
settlements, *USA Today*:

https://www.usatoday.com/story/news/nation/2014/09/29/phoenix-va-whistle-blowers-retaliation-settlements/16440425/

Fired Phoenix VA Chief Helman took secret gifts, *Arizona Republic*/AZ Central: https://www.azcentral.com/story/news/arizona/investigations/2014/12/23/va-phoenix-director-helman-appeal/20829097/

VA removes Sharon Helman, manager at the center of Phoenix Health Care scandal, *Washington Post*: https://www.washingtonpost.com/news/federal-eye/wp/2014/11/24/va-removes-sharon-helman-manager-at-center-of-phoenix-health-care-scandal/

Office of Special Counsel Testimony, April 13, 2015, Pedene, mentioned: https://osc.gov/Pages/SearchResults.aspx?k=Paula%20Pedene

Office of Special Counsel Testimony, July 30, 2015, Pedene mentioned: https://osc.gov/Documents/Resources/Congressional%20Matters/Congressional%20Testimony%20and%20Transcripts/Testimony%20of%20Special%20Counsel%20Carolyn%20Lerner%20on%20%E2%80%9CReview%20of%20Whistleblower%20Claims%20at%20the%20Department%20of%20Veterans%20Affairs,%E2%80%9D%20July%2030,%202015.pdf

Veterans rally to protest lack of progress in improving care, *PBS/Cronkite News*: https://cronkitenews.azpbs.org/2015/11/09/veterans-rally-at-va-medical-center-to-protest-lack-of-progress-in-improving-care/

VA's original whistleblower breaks her silence, *Yahoo News*: https://news.yahoo.com/phoenix-va-s-original-whistleblower-1325508524146742.html

A Talk with PR Pro of the Year, PRSA Strategist, Nov 2015: https://apps.prsa.org/Intelligence/TheStrategist/Articles/view/11334/1120/A_Talk_With_PR_Pro_of_the_Year_Paula_L_Pedene_APR#.YOueauhKg4t

A Q&A with PR Pro of the Year, bonus online article, PRSA: https://apps.prsa.org/SearchResults/view/11348/105/Bonus_Online_Article_Q_and_A_With_PR_Pro_of_the_Ye#.YOuewOhKg4t

Phoenix VA whistleblower wins top national honor, *Phoenix Business Journal*: https://www.bizjournals.com/phoenix/news/2015/11/03/phoenix-va-whistleblower-wins-top-national-pr.html

The Whistleblowers Story, a modern-day battle of David versus Goliath, IPRA: https://www.ipra.org/news/itle/itl-159-the-whistleblowers-story-a-modern-day-battle-of-david-versus-goliath/

Office of Special Counsel, Letter to the President, June 1, 2016: https://osc.gov/Documents/Public%20Files/FY16/DI-14-2839%20and%202975/DI-14-2839%20and%20DI-14-2975%20Letter%20to%20President.pdf

Former Phoenix VA Director Sharon Helman sentenced, *Arizona Republic*: https://www.azcentral.com/story/news/local/arizona-investigations/2016/05/16/former-phoenix-va-director-sharon-helman-sentenced/84452488/

One year later, the VA Wait Time Scandal, *Arizona Republic*/AZ Central: https://www.azcentral.com/story/news/politics/investigations/2015/04/10/one-year-later-va-scandal/25596795/

Executive Inc: Meet Paula Pedene, the former VA whistleblower, now leads Phoenix Veterans Day Parade: https://www.bizjournals.com/phoenix/news/2020/08/07/paula-pedene-organizes-phoenix-veterans-day-Parade.html

CPSIA information can be obtained
at www.ICGtesting.com
Printed in the USA
LVHW021557261121
704514LV00007B/18/J

9 781947 394049